# The Black College Mystique

JAN 2006

CH

# The Black College Mystique

Charles V. Willie
Richard J. Reddick
Ronald Brown

ROWMAN & LITTLEFIELD PUBLISHERS, INC.
*Lanham • Boulder • New York • Toronto • Oxford*

ROWMAN & LITTLEFIELD PUBLISHERS, INC.

Published in the United States of America
by Rowman & Littlefield Publishers, Inc.
A wholly owned subsidary of The Rowman & Littlefield Publishing Group, Inc.
4501 Forbes Boulevard, Suite 200, Lanham, Maryland 20706
www.rowmanlittlefield.com

PO Box 317
Oxford
OX2 9RU, UK

British Library Cataloguing in Publication Information Available

**Library of Congress Cataloging-in-Publication Data**

Willie, Charles Vert, 1927–
The black college mystique / Charles V. Willie, Richard J. Reddick, and Ronald Brown.
     p.   cm.
Includes bibliographical references and index.
ISBN 0-7425-4616-0 (cloth : alk. paper)—ISBN 0-7425-4617-9 (pbk. : alk. paper)
1. African Americans—Education (Higher)   2. African American universities and
colleges.   I. Reddick, Richard, 1972–   II. Brown, Ronald.   III. Title.
LC2781.W56 2006
378.73'08996073—dc22

                          2005017225


Printed in the United States of America

♾ ™ The paper used in this publication meets the minimum requirements of American
National Standard for Information Sciences—Permanence of Paper for Printed Library
Materials, ANSI/NISO Z39.48–1992.

This book is dedicated
to two esteemed graduates
of historically Black colleges and universities:

Lawrence Neal Jones, Dean Emeritus,
School of Religion, Howard University

and to the memory of his wife
Mary Ellen Jones, School Teacher

# Contents

# Acknowledgments

We acknowledge with appreciation permission to reprint as chapter 1 a revised version of "The Educational Goals of Black Colleges" by Charles V. Willie and Chester M. Hedgepeth Jr. first published in the *Journal of Higher Education* 50(1) (1979): 89–96.

We also acknowledge with appreciation permission to reprint as chapter 2 a revised version of "The Priorities of Presidents of Black Colleges" by Charles V. Willie and Marlene Y. MacLeish, first published in *Black Colleges in America,* ed. Charles V. Willie and Ronald R. Edmonds, 132–148 (Teachers College Press, 1978).

We acknowledge with appreciation permission to reprint as chapter 6 a revised version of "Black Colleges Redefined" by Charles V. Willie, first published in *Change* 11(7) (1979): 46–49.

Finally, we are grateful to the American Council on Education (ACE) for granting us permission to reanalyze a subset of data on historically Black colleges and universities (HBCUs) derived from its 2001 survey of public and private higher education institutions.

This book is the result of a study commissioned by the Southern Education Foundation, Inc. (SEF) as part of its program of assistance to HBCUs. The support from SEF, in part, was made possible through grants from the Charles Stewart Mott and Andrew W. Mellon Foundations.

In addition to expressing our appreciation to the American Council of Education (ACE) for permission to reanalyze its survey data, we are grateful to the SEF and especially Lynn Walker Huntley, its president, for recognizing the need to study HBCUs and their leaders. Dr. Joyce King, a staff member of the SEF when this study was conceived, facilitated our access to ACE data.

Dr. Leroy Davis, also a consultant to SEF when this study was launched, offered his wise perspective on the problems that Black college presidents confront. Dr. James Honan, a member of the faculty of the Harvard Graduate School of Education and a specialist in education finance and planning, gave sound advice on ways of designing a study of HBCU leaders. His advice is refined by information derived from annual visits to several private Black colleges during the past half decade or more with the senior author of this book. Dr. Honan read our entire manuscript and offered several valuable suggestions for chapter 7. We are grateful for the expert clerical and administrative support rendered by Nancy Bradley Capasso in preparing the manuscript for publication and the extraordinary support and wise advice offered by Grace Ebron of AltaMira Press.

We, the authors, take full responsibility for the analysis and interpretation of data presented in this study. The discussion in this book does not necessarily reflect the policy of any or our sponsoring or collaborating agencies or the universities with which the authors are affiliated.

# Preface

This report contains the results of our study of the unique combination of excellence and equity found in historically Black colleges and universities (HBCUs) in the United States. As stated by the philosopher and longshoreman Eric Hoffer in his book *The True Believer*, published a half century ago, the dominant people of power "play a large role in shaping a nation, but so do individuals at the other extreme" (the subdominant people of power) (Hoffer 1951, 24). If this statement be true, it is appropriate that all should take note of what is happening in Black colleges today for the guidance that such studies may offer for higher education in the future.

We know, for example, that free public schools available to all citizens of this republic was an idea that Thomas Jefferson had during the beginning years of the nineteenth century. However, this idea did not receive political support until after the Civil War. Black public officers who were elected to state legislatures during the Reconstruction gave strong support to proposals for free universal education financed by public funds. They believed, like Jefferson, that a democracy depends upon the capacity of citizens to understand common issues, analyze them, and arrive at sensible solutions after debate and negotiation. Thus, Black people tend to look upon education as a liberating experience that contributes to the public good by facilitating ethical and moral decision making on matters of public policy. White people tend to believe that universal education is the source of individual enhancement (a moral outcome), while Black people tend to believe that universal education is the fundamental source of group advancement as well as individual enhancement (ethical and moral outcomes).

The National Association for the Advancement of Colored People (NAACP) —representing subdominant people of power—launched a campaign in courts of law during the first half of the twentieth century to overcome racial segregation in public education that leaders of this organization believed hindered equality for people of color in the United States. During the second half of the twentieth century, dominant people of power—the majority—turned to education for personal cultivation and to help find one's "calling," one's proper niche in society that would lead to a feeling of self-fulfillment. Clearly, these two racial groups embraced education for similar and different reasons.

*The Almanac Issue* of *The Chronicle of Higher Education* published on August 29, 2003, reported that freshmen in four-year colleges (a cohort that is overwhelmingly White) had several personal reasons for going to college, most of which were for personal fulfillment.

After analyzing mission statements of several Black colleges and universities, Gregory Kannerstein found that "perhaps the greatest and most distinctive contribution of Black colleges to the American philosophy of higher education has been to emphasize and legitimate public community service as a major objective of colleges and universities." These colleges and universities define service in several ways such as responsiveness to the needs of the Black community in a specific locality, the state, or the nation; teaching racial understanding; and giving attention to ethical and moral values (Kannerstein 1978, 31).

In the discussion above, we see Whites emphasizing the value of education for what it can do for the individuals, including their moral development and personal success. Also, we see Blacks emphasizing the value of education for what it can do for the community, including the equitable distribution of goods, services, and opportunities to members of their group and others. The concluding words in Martin Buber's study of two types of faith—Judaism and Christianity—help to clarify the two approaches to education by Black people and White people in this nation. Judaism and Christianity, Buber said, "have something as yet unsaid to say to each other and a help to give to one another" (Buber 1951, 74). The exchange with one's opposite of new ideas and ways of doing things is something of value.

The written record on education of White people in this nation is plentiful, but not so for Black people and other people of color. Yet, Whites need to learn from Blacks and other people of color, just as these people need to learn from Whites about their common and different ways of solving educational and other social problems. We believe that both groups have something as yet unsaid to say to each other, and so does the Southern Education Foundation, Inc. (SEF).

After discussing the interests of the SEF in advancing equity and excellence in the South, we were invited to serve as consultants during 2003 to help the foundation identify ways of rendering specific help to four-year HBCUs.

The report we have prepared analyzes the composition and characteristics of the student body, faculty, and administration of Black colleges and relates these findings to the limited professional literature on this topic. Also, we examined the mission, goals, curriculum, and pedagogical methods and techniques used in Black colleges to enhance teaching and learning for their students and indicate ways in which these may benefit students in other population groups.

Finally, we analyze a sample of four-year private and public HBCUs using data from the 2001 survey of college presidents conducted by the American Council on Education (ACE). Our analysis covers the personal characteristics of Black college presidents, their alternative pathways to the status of chief executive officer, and some management matters that consume much of their time and about which they feel least prepared to confront. The book ends with a discussion of action strategies appropriate for presidents and boards of trustees in dealing with some of the problems that are troublesome to some Black colleges and their chief executive officers.

We believe the contents of this book may serve as a base for policy making within HBCUs and for foundations and government agencies that wish to render help. The findings should also be of interest to scholars in higher education administration, the sociology of education, the philosophy of education, race relations, and multicultural affairs.

Our overall finding is that HBCUs represent an important component of the higher education system in this nation and are essential to this system because of their innovative strategies for teaching all sorts and conditions of students, and also because of their existence as models of integrated learning environments, especially with reference to the racial and ethnic characteristics of teachers.

Mentoring is a magnificent skill found among staff and teachers in many Black colleges and universities. This skill and its implementation should be studied, understood, and replicated, if possible, in all institutions of higher education. For it is the direct participation in the life of students—serving them, sacrificing for them, and suffering with them—that generates trust and respect and the willingness for one to reach beyond his or her grasp.

# Introduction

# Five Secrets about Black Colleges Revealed in This Book

## 1. BLACK COLLEGES ARE NOT JUST FOR BLACK STUDENTS.

To say that Black colleges are not just for Black students is to acknowledge the importance of diversity and to recognize that the unique and effective teaching styles developed by many Black institutions of higher education could help others and should be available to all, including Whites, because their presence will not harm the integrity of historically Black colleges and universities (HBCUs), as the presence of Blacks has not harmed the integrity of traditionally White institutions (TWIs).

Our research and personal experience reveal that many preeminent schools in the United States have diversified their student bodies with good outcomes. More than one out of every three students admitted to the first-year class for the 2004–2005 school year at Harvard and Stanford are persons of color. The relatively large presence of people of color as a minority on the campuses of these and other venerable White institutions and of White students as a minority group in predominantly Black college learning environments will do no harm, as revealed by the record of such happenings. Actually, diversity is an enhancement phenomenon. Since an increasing number of White colleges now enroll Black students, Black colleges could benefit from enrollment strategies that will give them a greater market share of all college-going students. There are some economic as well as educational reasons that Black colleges should enroll non-Black students today.

Chapter 2 in this book indicates the special attention, care, and concern that Black colleges give to students who have great promise but some deficits in their precollege education. The presidents of HBCUs testify in chapter 2 that such persons, after receiving a Black college education, usually are able to "go on to graduate school and . . . make significant contributions to society." We know that some White students are in need of the unique care and concern that Black colleges offer. Julian Roebuck and Komanduri Murty studied White students who attended Black colleges in the Southeastern region of the United States in 1989 through 1991 and reported in their book *Historically Black Colleges and Universities* that a majority of White students enrolled in HBCUs said Black faculty members were "competent, fair, and helpful" and "viewed [Whites] as worthy students" (1993, 167). These findings as well as our research indicate that there is "a will" among some White students to attend predominantly Black colleges. What is missing is "the way"—a clear pathway that includes counseling staff on Black college campuses for White minority students, financial assistance, and recruitment strategies. Thus, we declare that Black colleges are not only for Black students, just as White colleges are not only for White students. Chapter 4 in this book discusses some of the good educational experiences that Whites have had at Black colleges. Chapter 2 also reports the observation of a Black college president that foundations have not offered grants to Black colleges to assist in the recruitment of White students, as in the 1960s and 1970s when foundations offered assistance to TWIs to recruit Black students.

Most Black college presidents declare that they had racially segregated Black student bodies in the past because of state-imposed law before the *Brown v. Board of Education* Supreme Court decision ruled that segregation has no place in public education; these presidents tell us that Black schools never were segregating institutions.

Thus, Roebuck and Murty conclude that "historically black colleges and universities continue to have a significant place in higher education in the United States." In light of information presented in chapters 6 and 7, we endorse this conclusion and further say HBCUs have a destiny with diversity (1993, 205).


## 2. HISTORICALLY BLACK COLLEGES AND UNIVERSITIES HAVE THE MOST DIVERSIFIED FACULTIES AMONG ALL INSTITUTIONS OF HIGHER EDUCATION.

According to the 2001 edition of the *Digest of Education Statistics,* in 1998 only 5.1 percent of faculty members and staff in all degree-granting institutions in the United States were Black. This proportion is significantly less than the 34 percent of Whites on the faculties of private Black colleges and universities during the closing decades of the twentieth century, according to a 1984 *Statistical Report* of the United Negro College Fund. Actually, the proportion of Whites on the faculty of Black schools is six to seven times larger than the proportion of Blacks on the faculty and staff of all schools. Within the past generation, the proportion of White faculty members in HBCUs has ranged from 40 percent, according to a 1975 report of the U.S. Equal Employment Opportunity Commission (EEOC), to 28 percent, according to Kenneth Jost (2003, 1047–1060).

Racial diversity in HBCU faculties is not new. During the beginning decades of the twentieth century, Whites constituted about two-thirds of Black college faculties, and most administrators of these schools were White. HBCUs also welcomed faculty refugees from Europe during and after World War II, when other institutions were reluctant to hire them. Black colleges continue to have a fair number of international teachers who were not born in the United States.

In addition to racial diversity, HBCUs have exhibited great diversity in gender characteristics of faculty members. *Barron's Profiles of American Colleges* (BES 1994) reports that Hampton University, a leader among Black schools, has a well-balanced faculty in regard to gender—52 percent female and 48 percent male. According to *The African American Education Data Book* (1997), Hampton is not alone. The regular full-time faculty of all HBCUs is well balanced (50 percent male and 50 percent female). This experience for all HBCUs is different from the distribution of faculty members by gender in all degree-granting institutions in the United States in which men are 64 percent and women are 36 percent, according to the 2001 edition of the *Digest of Education Statistics.*

HBCUs experienced the value of faculty diversity early on and should have some wisdom to share with other institutions of higher education, including TWIs, since the Supreme Court in *Grutter v. Bollinger* (2003) has recognized the essentiality of diversity in the educational mission of schools. The benefits of diversity that HBCUs have learned are discussed in chapter 1 in a treatise on the concepts "double culture," "double consciousness," and "double victory" and in chapters 3 and 4. Black colleges are well positioned because of their long history of accommodating a pluralistic faculty to help other institutions of higher education learn how to achieve unity out of diversity and a sense of community among people from different cultural heritages.

## 3. BLACK COLLEGE ADMINISTRATORS TEND TO BELIEVE THAT A COLLEGE IS NO BETTER THAN ITS FACULTY.

Benjamin Elijah Mays, former president of Morehouse College, the spiritual mentor of Martin Luther King Jr., and one of the nation's most esteemed educators, stated repeatedly his belief that a college is no better than its faculty.

This was his mantra. To perform their awesome responsibilities, Mays wanted Black colleges to recruit faculties well equipped with expert knowledge and with wisdom that is based on good, practical judgment.

Wisdom is a many-splendored thing—magnificent, inspiring, enlightening, and reflective. Wise teachers develop empathetic relationships with all students, meet each student where he or she is regarding previous education, and mentor students with great expectations and generous support. A learning environment consisting of these relationships enables students to transcend the constraints of personal conditions of life and to transform defective institutional arrangements for the purpose of achieving a more perfect community that enhances the life chances of all.

Blacks are more concerned with what students take away from college than what they bring to it. Thus, Black colleges are inclined to give a chance to some students whom other schools reject. Several years ago, Virginia Union University in Richmond, Virginia, published these words in its catalog: "Entering qualifications of the students . . . are important, but they are secondary to the qualifications of the graduating student."

To redeem some students from a life of apathy and to stimulate what seems to be a magical change in their life course, extraordinary teachers in Black colleges effectively educate ordinary students by serving them, sacrificing for them, and suffering with them.

Thus, Black colleges boast not about the high average Scholastic Aptitude Test (SAT) scores and other indicators of good scholarship among students accepted for the first-year class. Such schools are more pleased and impressed with the cultivated growth, development, and promise of students when they graduate. Embracement of characteristics of graduating students as indicators of the reputation of a school is a fundamental difference in the belief systems of leaders of HBCUs and leaders of TWIs. Among leaders of the latter group, characteristics of entering students are used as reputational indicators of school quality. These issues are discussed in detail in chapters 2, 3, and 4 and lead to the conclusion that a higher education system in the United States that had a Harvard but not a Hampton would be incomplete, as mentioned in chapter 6.

## 4. BLACK COLLEGES HAVE A TWOFOLD MISSION OF INDIVIDUAL ENHANCEMENT AND COMMUNITY ADVANCEMENT.

In teaching one how to advance the community while, at the same time, to enhance the individual, Black colleges acknowledge the need for both excellence and equity (not one or the other but both) as goals to achieve in higher education. In chapters 4 and 6, Gregory Kannerstein mentions the legitimacy that Black colleges have given to participation in community advancement activities. This is a major contribution in a nation that increasingly emphasizes personal fulfillment and individual enhancement.

Charles Willie's career study titled *Five Black Scholars* (1986) revealed that quality scholarship (an excellence factor) is one important reason for labeling an educator as outstanding. This was the opinion of Blacks as well as Whites. Despite excellent scholarship, Blacks, in their hierarchy of values, would not designate good scholars as outstanding unless they also made a significant contribution to the community for the purpose of uplifting it.

Community uplift may be classified as an equity variable, and quality scholarship, as mentioned above, is an excellence variable. Blacks recognize the complexity of higher education by insisting that excellence and equity go together and are complementary. One without the other is incomplete.

The 2002 annual national survey of attitudes of freshmen students in four-year colleges by the Higher Education Research Institute (HERI) at the University of California in Los Angeles and published in the 2003–2004 almanac issue of the *Chronicle of Higher Education* reveals that 70 percent or more first-year college students decided to go to college for these reasons: to learn more about themselves, to be able to get a better job, to get training for a specific career, and to be able to make more money (CHE 2003, 17). The population studied was predominantly White. Thus, these responses may be considered, by and large, as the main reasons most White students go to college. All of the reasons may be classified under the personal fulfillment category.

These reasons would be insufficient from the perspective of Black educators who were discussed in *Five Black Scholars*. They believed that education should help a person to develop capacities to help others as well as to help oneself. Thus, Blacks, as a population, and Black colleges have kept alive the importance of community advancement as a basic interest of educated people. We should congratulate Black colleges for continuing to emphasize equity issues and draw these to the attention of educated people. Black colleges do this because they realize that the pursuit of equity does not detract from the pursuit of excellence.

As noted in chapter 2, Hugh Gloster, a Black college president, called Martin Luther King Jr., a Black college graduate, the archetype of an educated person—one who combined academic and professional success with personal integrity and social concern. Gloster believed that the life of Martin Luther King Jr. was worthy of emulation by all, and so do we!

## 5. BLACK COLLEGES ARE, HAVE BEEN, AND WILL CONTINUE TO BE PART OF THE HIGHER EDUCATION MAINSTREAM.

Back in 1967, Christopher Jencks and David Riesman, two faculty members of Harvard University, wrote a damning critique of Black colleges in the United States. The critique, which appeared in the thirty-seventh volume of the *Harvard Educational Review,* labeled Black colleges as "academic disaster areas" and declared that they marched at the end of the educational parade, as mentioned in chapters 2 and 6.

Nearly a decade later, Riesman disavowed his earlier position, declaring to a reporter of the *Philadelphia Evening Bulletin* that he had "rethought" it and that both he and Black colleges had changed. Nevertheless, the damage was done. In effect, the Jencks-Riesman article located Black colleges outside the mainstream of higher education in the United States.

Black college presidents fought back. One said, "Black colleges are and have been a national resource." Another said, "The product of Black colleges provide a unique, essential and priceless ingredient [in] American society that the nation can no longer do without nor afford to neglect" (Willie and MacLeish 1978, 138–140).

While all metaphors are of limited value in describing human social organization, they do help us to better visualize some relationships. If education as an institution in society is the mainstream, it continues to be a useful gushing river developing and disseminating knowledge because of the many different tributaries that flow into it. The mainstream, therefore, is a composition of waters from all of its tributaries. In human society, these tributaries may be identified as multiple cultural groups such as Black, Brown, and White racial groups; lower-class, middle-class and upper-class socioeconomic groups; Spanish-speaking, Cajun-speaking, and Yiddish-speaking linguistic groups; Catholic, Protestant, and Muslim religious groups; and so on. Unique cultural ingredients flow out of these tributaries and are assimilated in the mainstream. Thus, it is inappropriate for any particular cultural tributary group to claim total ownership of the mainstream.

Moreover, because the mainstream depends upon its tributaries, it is always in a state of flux. Even a cultural tributary group such as the majority cannot lay claim to the mainstream because it is not the only cultural tributary group that makes a contribution to the mainstream.

Finally, once a cultural group makes a contribution to the mainstream, it cannot withdraw the contribution and it cannot determine how that contribution will be assimilated with contributions from other sources and used.

Thus, the Black college president who said, "Black colleges provide a unique, essential and priceless ingredient [in] American society" was correct

(Willie and MacLeish 1978, 147–148). So was the Black lawyer who said, "White Americans owe a debt of gratitude to Black Americans for making the Constitution work" (William T. Coleman, qtd. in Willie and Edmonds 1978, 3). And so was the White sociologist who correctly observed that "it is not infrequently the case that the non-conforming minority in a society represents the interests and ultimate values of the group more effectively than the conforming majority" (Merton 1968, 421). These observations suggest that the mainstream belongs to all of us, because all of us have made a contribution to it.

A classic example that all have contributed to the mainstream and that the mainstream belongs to all of us is the Civil Rights Act of 1964. Joseph L. Rauh, an attorney and vice chair of the Americans for Democratic Action, along with Clarence Mitchell Jr., director of the Washington Office of the National Association for the Advancement of Colored People, were two of the chief lobbyists for the Civil Rights Act of 1964. Rauh attributes the decisive effect upon the U.S. Congress and its affirmative vote for this civil rights legislation to Martin Luther King Jr. and the demonstrations for civil rights in Birmingham, Alabama that he and others led in 1963. This congressional act called for the elimination of racial discrimination in employment and the rapid increase and promotion of groups traditionally underrepresented. Affirmative action of this sort was also applied to admission practices of colleges and universities.

The affirmative action program at the Davis Campus Medical School of the University of California from 1971 to 1974 set aside sixteen of one hundred medical school seats for African Americans and other minorities. White students could compete for only eighty-four of the one hundred seats in the first-year class of medical school during these years, because sixteen were reserved for Blacks and other people of color. Theoretically, however, Blacks and other students of color could compete for all of the one hundred seats; indeed, they received thirteen of the remaining eighty-four seats according to Allan P. Sindler's report in *Bakke, Defunis, and Minority Admissions* (1978). The school was trying to fulfill requirements of the Civil Rights Act of 1964 by guaranteeing seats in the entering class for a group that, traditionally, had been underrepresented.

Title VI of the Civil Rights Act of 1964 that called for the elimination of racial discrimination in employment was the public law used by Alan Bakke, a White male college graduate with a good undergraduate record, who was rejected twice by the University of California, Davis, School of Medicine. The Supreme Court in 1978 declared that Bakke had been excluded because of race and ordered the UCDavis School of Medicine to admit him. It did, and he graduated with an MD degree. This summary of what happened in the Bakke case was included in Robert D. Loevy's *The Civil Rights Act of 1964* (1997, 346–348).

An important point to remember is that the Civil Rights Act was passed, in part, because of the civil rights movement. And Alan Bakke, a White person, used Title VI of the law to support his claim for enrollment in the UCDavis School of Medicine. The *Bakke* case demonstrates that the mainstream (which includes federal laws) belongs to everyone even though the intent of a law may have been for the purpose of dealing with discriminatory experiences of people of color and to respond to the civil rights movement mounted by them to redress their grievances. People of color who mobilized and brought pressure on their government to do the right thing represented a tributary that flowed into the mainstream and had a major effect upon it that benefited the people from the majority-oriented tributary as well as people connected with a minority-oriented tributary. Thus, Alan Bakke used the Civil Rights Act of 1964 to redress his grievances. In all chapters of this book and especially chapters 5 and 7, Black people and their institutions such as Black colleges are described as full participants in the mainstream with unique offerings for the mainstream derived from their minority experience.

*Part I*

# PERCEPTIONS, PROBLEMS, AND POSSIBILITIES OF HISTORICALLY BLACK COLLEGES AND UNIVERSITIES A GENERATION AGO

*Chapter One*

# Educational Goals of Black Colleges

Black colleges and universities are relatively young as the years of institutions are numbered. Some are more than a century old, but most are younger—only two to four scores of years in age. From the beginning, Black schools have struggled against heavy odds and severe criticism. In *The Souls of Black Folk,* W. E. B. Du Bois wrote that after the Civil War, the first major attempt to educate Blacks "showed itself in ashes, insult and blood." He said that "opposition to Negro education in the south was . . . bitter" (Du Bois 1903, 32). Nevertheless, predominantly Black schools such as Morehouse College, Fisk University, Atlanta University, Howard University, and Hampton Institute were founded during the immediate post–Civil War period with public and private assistance from the Freedmen's Bureau, national religious organizations, and other groups. These schools have endured.

Not all Black schools achieved the reputations of those mentioned. Some of the Black colleges founded before the twentieth century, according to Du Bois, "were . . . worthy of ridicule" (1903, 44). They did the best they could do with what they had. But in the opinion of Du Bois, this was not enough. Thus, from the very beginning, some Black schools were ridiculed or opposed by Blacks as well as Whites. Such an experience prompted one of the authors to state elsewhere that life for the Black college president, in the words of Langston Hughes, "ain't been no crystal stair" (Willie and MacLeish 1978, 132).

The criticism and ridicule has not abated. During the mid-twentieth century, Ralph Ellison ridiculed a Black college in Alabama in his book *The Invisible*

Acknowledged with appreciation is the support for this research from the Center for Minority Group Mental Health Program in the National Institute for Mental Health. This chapter was written by Charles V. Willie and Chester M. Hedgepeth Jr. and first published in the *Journal of Higher Education* 50(1) (1979): 89–96, and is republished with permission.

*Man* (1952). Howard Zinn characterized Black college presidents as following "the traditions of conservatism and moderation" (Zinn 1970, 120). The most stunning insult came from David Riesman and Christopher Jencks, who called Black colleges collectively "academic disaster areas" (Riesman and Jencks 1968, 68). Benjamin E. Mays rebutted these criticisms and said that they were "subtle moves . . . to abolish Black colleges" (Mays 1971, 192). The attacks that surrounded the establishment of Black colleges after the Civil War have continued to plague these schools after the civil rights movement of the twentieth century. As a result, Black colleges have been on the defensive, always justifying why they should exist.

Zinn stated that "perhaps the Negro is the last guardian of a moral reservoir from which the entire nation may some day drink" (Zinn 1970, 125). This moral dimension of education is ignored by most of the detractors of Black colleges because they do not understand it.

Jencks and Riesman, for example, indicated a lack of understanding of the academic value of moral and ethical education when they stated that "Any Negro college anxious to investigate the question of academic 'value added' can . . . do so rather easily . . . by seeing whether the majority of its students improved their percentile ranks or reduced it when [the] 'verbal scores' of seniors on the Graduate Record Examination are compared with those on the Scholastic Aptitude Test taken before entering college" (qtd. in Wright et al. 1967, 467). Their concept of "value added" by a college education is so narrowly defined that it completely ignores the contribution of moral and ethical values and the development of several other intelligences in a college education.

The purpose of this discussion is not to defend Black colleges but to indicate what they do that is unique and of benefit to other institutions of higher education.

Because Black colleges in the past have been preoccupied with defending their right to exist, they have not had the privilege of fully explaining their educational goals and methods from which others might benefit. This discussion is an effort in that direction, an explication of the norms that guide the educational experiences provided by predominantly Black colleges. S. M. Nabrit said, "The liberals who perceive everything in terms of White norms and values may be the worst enemy of the Negro institutions" (Nabrit 1971, 661). What then are the norms and values that Black colleges seek to achieve?

It is important for Black colleges to recognize that their contribution has been not for the benefit of Blacks only but for the good of the entire system of higher education in this nation. Such recognition will strengthen these institutions to withstand attempts to close or remake them in the image of White colleges. The Black-college experience is a unique one in higher education that ought to be preserved, refined, and shared.

This experience has done three things for higher education: (1) it has continued to expose students to a double culture, (2) it has helped students to develop a double consciousness, and (3) it has taught students to seek a double victory. The ideas of double culture, double consciousness, and double victory are important and deserve a more detailed discussion. Black colleges have not been cut off from the diverse cultures in this country. Since their inception, these institutions have invited White and Brown scholars to teach and direct programs on their campuses. Students and faculties have benefited from these cross-cultural experiences. There is hardly a Black college today without a sizable Brown and White faculty and staff. The task is to preserve this special quality of racial cooperation. Most Black administrators maintain campuses consisting of diversified faculties in terms of race because they recognize the beneficial effects of a multicultural environment based on their own education, particularly their graduate education in predominantly White schools. One of America's most distinguished educators, Benjamin Mays, said that his matriculation at predominantly White Bates College was the experience that dismissed from his mind for all time the myth of the inherent superiority of Whites. Mays said that he had objective proof through the competitive experience at Bates that he, although Black, "had done better in academic performances, in public speaking, and in argumentation and debate than the vast majority of [his] classmates" (qtd. in Willie 1973, 31).

James Coleman found "that Blacks in an integrated school gain a better sense of control of their destinies . . . due to the fact that they see that they can do some things better than Whites and can perform in school better than some Whites, a knowledge which they never had so long as they were isolated in an all Black school" (Coleman 1968, 25).

W. E. B. Du Bois and Martin Luther King Jr. have stated that the African roots and the American experience have created a double consciousness in Blacks, a strength that enables them to adapt and to learn far more readily than individuals who possess single perspectives of their identity. For example, King said that the Black American "is neither totally African nor totally Western. He is Afro-American, a true hybrid, a combination of two cultures," and therefore has a sympathetic understanding of both groups of people (King 1968b, 61). Because of this circumstance, we classify Blacks as double-cultured people who have empathetic relationships with people in a large number of different cultural groups.

King made significant observations on the need for a double victory during the freedom and civil rights movements. Regarding the necessity of Black and White cooperation, King stated that "there is no separate Black path to power and fulfillment that does not intersect White paths, and there is no separate White path to power and fulfillment, short of social disaster, that does not share that power with Black aspirations for freedom and human dignity" (King 1968b, 60–61).

The double victory that is King's constructive ethic derives from, and is the consummation of, the double-culture and double-consciousness concepts. After segregated seating on city buses was declared unconstitutional by the Supreme Court in 1956, the Montgomery Improvement Association, led by Martin Luther King Jr., that coordinated the boycott of segregated buses prepared a list titled "Suggestions for Integrating Buses." Two of the suggestions were manifestations of the double-victory concept. Item 6 on the list reminded Black people that "this is not a victory for Negroes alone, but for all Montgomery and the South. Do not boast! Do not brag!" Item 7 admonished Blacks to "be loving enough to absorb evil and understanding enough to turn an enemy into a friend" (King 1958, 144). These recommendations are anchored in the double-victory concept. These three concepts—double culture, double consciousness, and double victory—are discussed below in terms of their application to Black colleges and universities.

## DOUBLE CULTURE

The ghetto existence for Blacks in the past has been a living example of unity out of diversity. Residential segregation by race and ethnicity has characterized U.S. society at large; Black ghettos have consisted of people who are poor and affluent, often living side by side. The benefit of this togetherness is that both groups see each other, talk with each other, and become friends. The dialogue and association have resulted in genuine communication and caring across the social classes despite racial isolation in the ghetto.

The Black college campus that draws its students from the Black communities of this nation is reflective of the religious and socioeconomic diversity of Blacks. Thus, Black college campuses consist of poor and affluent people, the dispossessed and the well connected. Such diversity tends to prevent the development of social class stereotypes among Black people.

Black colleges know that ability is more or less randomly distributed within its population and that limited opportunity often results in limited achievement until teachers and students together find ways of overcoming the impediments and limitations of the past. Teachers know this because they see students daily from impoverished backgrounds becoming scholars and leaders on campus. The direct association between students of varying socioeconomic circumstances on the Black college campus has enriched their knowledge and understanding of a wider range of human nature. Such knowledge and understanding are different from that obtained indirectly about people whom one has not seen and does not know. Thus, the coming together of a variety of students on the Black college campus is a pedagogical as well as a humanistic experience recommended for all colleges and universities. Majority as well as minority populations will benefit from experiencing racial, ethnic, and socioeconomic diversity. Black colleges have pioneered in maintaining college campuses with diversified student bodies with respect to socioeconomic status and other conditions of life.

The requirement for the future is that Black colleges and all institutions of higher education should attract students whose presence will result in student bodies that are diversified. Already, these colleges have demonstrated the value of bringing together faculty members of differing racial, religious, and socioeconomic backgrounds. Now they must demonstrate the educational benefits of bringing together students from Black, Brown, and White communities. Education is for the purpose of enlarging the perspectives of students beyond the customs and conventions of their folk community. These widened perspectives should include cosmopolitan concerns of this country and of the world at large. Black colleges have integrated very well teachers of different racial groups. They now must find ways of achieving racial diversity within their student bodies. An education received in isolation is deficient because it lacks the enrichment of multicultural perspectives.

A study of publicly supported Black colleges in 1975 reveals that one out of every ten students in these schools is White (Willie and MacLeish 1978, 98). Private Black colleges are ready to diversify their student bodies but have received little assistance from foundations and other sources that could provide funds for the attraction of White students to their campus. Hugh Gloster, former president of Morehouse College, points out that Black schools have sought funds to recruit White students but have not received any assistance. Indeed he said, "I know of no predominantly Black college that has received a large grant providing scholarship money to attract White students" (Willie and MacLeish 1978, 96–97). In the 1960s, significant foundations such as Rockefeller and Ford made a series of grants to predominantly White institutions such as Duke, Emory, Tulane, Vanderbilt, Antioch, Carleton, Grinnell, Oberlin, Occidental, Reed, and Swarthmore to help them recruit minority students. Now is the time to offer predominantly Black institutions of higher education similar assistance in recruiting White students.

The basic benefits of education in a predominantly Black college setting need not be eroded by including Whites in the student body. Whites would enhance the educational experience, as have affluent and poor people when educated together. Whites who come to a predominantly Black college must come to be enriched by the Black experience, just as Blacks who enroll in a predominantly White college are enriched by the White experience. It is not the Black or White culture alone that is of intrinsic value but the presence of the two or more cultures on a campus that enhances the education of all. Each culture has something to give and take from the other.

## DOUBLE CONSCIOUSNESS

The concept of double consciousness has been explored by several social scientists, including W. E. B. Du Bois. In race relations, Du Bois has this to say about double consciousness: "It is a peculiar sensation, this double consciousness, this sense of always looking at one's self through the eyes of others, of measuring one's soul by the tape of a world that looks on in amused contempt and pity. One ever feels his two-ness—an American, a Negro; two souls, two thoughts, two unreconciled strivings." Du Bois did not wish to eliminate the double consciousness, although he called it "a peculiar sensation." His wish was that it should be possible "for a man [or woman] to be both a Negro and an American" (Du Bois 1903, 3), a synthesis that could occur during one's educational odyssey.

While Du Bois spoke of Blacks in the United States, it is clear that his concept of double consciousness could be generalized as an outcome of minority status in any common culture whose majority is more powerful and different from the minority. It is fair to say that double consciousness is probably more often a property of subdominant and less powerful members in a social organization. This status requires the examination of one's status and role from one's own perspective and from the perspective of others as a means of survival. Persons with limited resources must understand and outmaneuver people who are more powerful if the powerful are not compassionate.

The responsibilities of minorities and majorities or dominant and subdominant people of power are quite different. As minorities in the United States, Black students have insisted that this nation live up to its principles and fulfill its laws pertaining to freedom, justice, and equality. However, no society functions properly if run only according to law. Every society needs some people who are generous, who give more than they are required to give. Generosity is possible only among people who control resources. None is required to give more than one's fair share. Yet, a society cannot operate effectively unless some people are generous and magnanimous, giving more than they were required to give and taking less than they are entitled to receive. The dominant people of power who control community resources must learn to be generous for the common good. And the subdominant people of power must learn how to love an imperfect world (Kushner 1981, 147–148) while trying to transform it. This action may involve voluntarily taking less than one is entitled, thus being magnanimous for the common good.

Magnanimity, a property of minority status, and generosity, a property of majority status, complement each other in human society. Because all may become members of the minority or the majority in a democracy, it is important to learn how to adapt to the requirements of a position and to fulfill its many possible roles. Blacks who seldom have been in control need to learn how to be genuinely generous when they are in charge. Whites who are not used to being dependent on people of color need to learn how to function in a magnanimous way, to take less than they are entitled to receive for the common good when they are not in charge.

Every predominantly Black college ought to have a White or Brown minority population that is sufficiently large to require the adaptive behavior of generosity and compassion by the Black majority. This can occur only if Whites seek out opportunities to be the minority. There are lessons to be learned as a minority that are necessary for an effective adaptation to life and all of its contingencies. The double consciousness enables the minority people to see themselves as they are and as they are perceived by the majority. It is well that members of a majority population experience minority status at some period during their education. Also, it is of value that all minorities should become the majority at some period in their education. By exchanging positions, each group may understand the necessity of magnanimity and courage as well as generosity and compassion in human society. Black colleges have helped some White people (especially teachers) develop a double consciousness by receiving them on campus as the minority. Whites who have experienced minority status will benefit from this experience by developing a double consciousness and greater empathy.

## DOUBLE VICTORY

A college education for Blacks never has been a self-centered thing. It has been for the purpose of helping others. In seeking the uplift of Blacks, one must at the same time seek the uplift of Whites and others. Essentially, this is the message that characterized the civil rights movement led by Martin Luther King Jr. and others. In seeking victory for one's own group, one has to seek victory for the total society. This is what King called the double victory, the turning of an enemy into a friend. Black colleges that have nurtured this concept should help other institutions of higher education understand that there is no justice for anyone unless there is justice for everyone.

The double victory involves mutual fulfillment. There is no victor or vanquished but a new synthesis and harmonic whole. Thus, the justice that Black colleges seek embraces Blacks, Browns, and Whites. The freedom about which Black colleges teach is for the purpose of liberating the majority as well as minorities.

By keeping alive in their students knowledge and understanding of the double culture, the double consciousness, and the double victory, Black colleges have made a unique and major contribution to higher education in this country. They, in fact, have demonstrated the validity of these educational goals for all.

# Chapter Two

# Priorities of Black College Presidents

Nobody knows the trouble I see;
Nobody knows but Jesus.
Nobody knows the trouble I see;
Glory Hallelujah!

Stanza from an old spiritual

Spirituals were developed in response to the circumstances of a slave but could have been written for the president of a Black college. "Nobody knows the trouble I see" expresses a feeling of aloneness and despair. "Glory Hallelujah!" is affirmation of hope. Between these two moods swings the administrative practice of presidents of Black colleges. The problems they deal with are severe. The support they receive is scant. Their success has been sure but unsteady. Yet they—and their schools—have managed to endure, overcome, and survive because they have faced adversity with ingenuity and continued to hope.

To provide a historical context for the contemporary analysis of Black colleges and their leaders in parts II and III, we present in this chapter a historical analysis of these schools a generation or more ago.

The famous Fisk Jubilee Singers were an ingenious creation of a Black college administrator. Shortly after Fisk University was founded in 1866, lack of money was a perplexing problem for the administration; the school's closing seemed inevitable. It was the ingenious idea of the treasurer to organize a singing group of students. He predicted that its inspiring renditions of slave

Written by Charles V. Willie, Harvard University, and Marlene Y. MacLeish, Morehouse Medical School, and first published in Charles Willie and Ronald R. Edmonds, eds., *Black Colleges in America* (Teachers College Press, 1978). This revised version is reproduced with permission.

spirituals would attract the public's attention and stimulate help for the new school. In October of 1871, the Jubilee Singers left the campus for a tour of the United States and Europe. They returned in 1878 with the money necessary to save the school and, according to John W. Work, "created over the world interest in [Black] education and in the spirituals" (Work 1940, 17).

To this day, Black college administrators have continued to be ingenious, pragmatic, and hopeful. They take what they have and use it well to do what they must. In his autobiography, Benjamin E. Mays describes his stewardship of twenty-seven years as president of Morehouse College with the words "so much with so little and so few" (Mays 1971, 170).

Notwithstanding their historical endurance, Mays said that he saw "a subtle move afloat to abolish Black colleges" at the beginning of the 1970s. He believed that "numerous critics" were part of a crusade to tear the Black college apart (Mays 1971, 192). Black college presidents have been the targets of critical scrutiny and ridicule in this attack. Christopher Jencks and David Riesman, for example, charged that many Black colleges are run "as if they were the personal property of their presidents" (Jencks and Riesman 1967, 48–49). Ann Jones, a White professor who taught at a Black college only two semesters, describes the president of her institution as a "paternalistic dictator" (Jones 1973, 119). However, Tobe Johnson, a Black professor of political science, acknowledged that "Black college presidents probably resemble the autocratic officials." But, he explained, such chief executives, "serving as the mediator between the college and the threatening environment, found it necessary to consolidate and maintain personal control over [their] organization" (Johnson 1971, 801).

Thus, the hostile, threatening, and nonsupportive environmental conditions surrounding Black colleges are related to the administrative styles of some of their leaders. It is a principle of political science that the more hostile and threatening the environment, the easier it is to legitimate the centralization of power. Johnson further states, "It can be argued that strong personal authority was essential to . . . survival" (Johnson 1971, 801). The resources of Black colleges have been so meager and their margin for error so small that administrators believe they cannot risk mistakes.

Most presidents, fully in control, do not seek power for self-serving purposes. Albert Dent, former president of Dillard University, emphasized that the presidents of Black colleges "are constantly seeking means by which to improve the effectiveness of their faculties" (Wright et al. 1967, 464). Mays, upon becoming president of Morehouse College in 1940, extracted a promise from the board of trustees (apparently a condition of his accepting the presidency) to raise the salary scale of the faculty (Mays 1971, 171). Black college presidents have remained visibly in control, but their control has been for the sake of preserving their institutions. Johnson reminds us, moreover, that they had good role models in the "autocratic officials who presided at the prestigious White schools during the nineteenth century" (Johnson 1971, 800).

## PROFILE OF BLACK COLLEGES

In 1967 when Jencks and Riesman published their study "The American Negro College" in the *Harvard Educational Review,* they stated that Black colleges tend to be small—"only one or two enroll more than 1,000 students, and most have fewer than 500. As a result, they operate with a faculty of 20 or 30 . . . and a budget of perhaps half a million dollars" (Jencks and Riesman 1967, 48).

The study by Willie and MacLeish in 1976 revealed quite a different picture. The purpose of this research was to provide Black college presidents with an opportunity to speak for themselves. It produced data supplied by presidents of twenty-one four-year schools that are members of the National Association for Equal Opportunity in Higher Education (NAFEO).[1] For fifteen colleges, we have statistical information about the institution plus information in narrative form. Table 2.1 lists the institutions participating, their location, and the names of the college presidents at that time.

Statistical data in table 2.2 reveal that the average size of the student body in these fifteen black colleges is 2,800. Only five of fifteen of the schools have student bodies under 1,000, and all of these have enrollments of over 500. The average size of the full-time faculty is 154; only three of the fifteen colleges have faculties with fewer than 50 members. The total budgets for the schools range from $1.8 million to $28.6 million, with an average of $9.9 million. Their average instructional budget is $4.1 million. None has a total budget, or even an instructional budget, of less than $500,000.

The Black colleges and universities in this study a generation ago are multimillion dollar educational enterprises and a major source of Black employment in some communities. Their full-time employees range in number from 100 to 2,000; the median is 213. Many of these multimillion dollar organizations are presided over by presidents of humble origin. They were born in such places as Eatonville, Florida; Middlesex County, Virginia; Telfair County, Georgia; Lumberton, Mississippi; Marion, Alabama; Eastover, South Carolina; and

---

[1]The National Association for Equal Opportunity in Higher Education (NAFEO) is an organization of public and private colleges and universities with student bodies that are predominantly Black. It is based in Silver Springs, Maryland. This association of two-year and four-year colleges and professional schools coordinates the response of these institutions to proposed public policies.

**Table 2.1.  Institutions participating in investigation of status of Black colleges, 1976**

| Institution | Location | President |
|---|---|---|
| Schools sending statistical data and narrative explanations. | | |
| Cheney State College | Cheney, PA | Wade Wilson |
| Florida A&M University | Tallahassee, FL | Benjamin L. Perry |
| Florida Memorial College | Miami, FL | Willie J. Wright |
| Federal City College | Washington, DC | Wendell Russell |
| Fort Valley State College | Fort Valley, GA | Cleveland Pettigrew |
| Huston-Tillotson College | Austin, TX | John T. King |
| Knoxville College | Knoxville, TN | Robert H. Harvey |
| LeMoyne-Owen College | Memphis, TN | Walter L. Walker |
| Morgan State University | Baltimore, MD | Andrew Billingsley |
| North Carolina A&T State University | Greensboro, NC | Lewis C. Dowdy |
| Paine College | Augusta, GA | Julius Scott |
| Paul Quinn College | Waco, TX | Stanley E. Rutland |
| Prairie View A&M University | Prairie View, TX | Alvin I. Thomas |
| Rust College | Holly Springs, MS | W. A. McMillan |
| Saint Augustine's College | Raleigh, NC | Prezell R. Robinson |
| Schools sending narrative explanations. | | |
| Bennett College | Greensboro, NC | Isaac H. Miller |
| Delaware State College | Dover, DW | Luna L. Mishoe |
| Elizabeth City State University | Elizabeth City, NC | Marion D. Thorpe |
| Tuskegee Institute | Tuskegee, AL | Luther H. Foster |
| Morehouse College | Atlanta, GA | Hugh M. Gloster |
| Spelman College | Atlanta, GA | Albert E. Manley |

Marsh Branch, North Carolina. Some could not have conceived of a million dollars in the days of their youth. Now they are overseeing sums of this magnitude and greater, and the stewardship of most of these leaders has been extraordinary, as the facts show.

How could Black colleges and universities change so rapidly if they were indeed "academic disaster areas" when Jencks and Riesman (1967, 26) wrote about them in the late 1960s? Our conclusion is that their assessment was off the mark then and now. Black colleges and universities, quite to the contrary, are a vital national resource. They have pioneered in providing higher education for young people, many of whom are associated with families of limited income. They have developed unique and extraordinary methods of instruction for students with deficits in precollege formal education.

**Table 2.2.  Data on students, faculty, and finances for fifteen Black colleges, 1976**

| Institution | Student Body | | | | Budget | | | Faculty | | | Full-Time Employees | Tuition and Fees |
|---|---|---|---|---|---|---|---|---|---|---|---|---|
| | Blacks | | Non-Blacks | Total | Total | Instructional | | Full-Time | With Doctorate | | | |
| Cheney State College* | 2,185 | (81) | 515 (19) | 2,700 | $13,000,000 | $8,000,000 | (62) | 188 | 68 | (36) | 401 | $750 |
| Florida A&M University* | 4,934 | (92) | 70 (8) | 5,404 | 13,763,292 | 5,715,864 | (42) | 399 | 155 | (38) | 2,092 | 476 |
| Florida Memorial College* | 600 | (100) | 0 (0) | 600 | 3,000,000 | 508,312 | (17) | 52 | 12 | (23) | 114 | 1,200 |
| Federal City College* | 7,552 | (92) | 650 (8) | 8,202 | 23,800,000 | 12,400,000 | (52) | 387 | 125 | (32) | 1,100 | ND‡ |
| Fort Valley State College* | 1,800 | (90) | 200 (10) | 2,000 | 7,000,000 | 4,000,000 | (57) | 152 | 65 | (43) | 395 | 460 |
| Huston-Tillotson College† | 584 | (85) | 104 (15) | 688 | ND | 2,646,403 | (84) | 46 | 17 | (37) | 141 | ND |
| Knoxville College† | 1,029 | (98) | 16 (2) | 1,045 | ND | ND | — | 57 | 23 | (40) | 182 | 930 |
| LeMoyne-Owen College† | 1,100 | (99.3) | 8 (0.7) | 1,108 | 2,514,000 | 1,260,000 | (50) | 58 | 25 | (43) | 155 | 975 |
| Morgan State University* | 5,532 | (87) | 829 (13) | 6,361 | 16,710,000 | 5,889,676 | (35) | 281 | 100 | (36) | 753 | 200 |
| North Carolina A&T University | 4,970 | (91) | 475 (9) | 5,345 | 11,842,000 | 6,123,979 | (52) | 307 | 134 | (43) | 1,009 | 798 |
| Paine College† | 767 | (99.3) | 6 (0.7) | 773 | 3,978,942 | 1,089,628 | (28) | 51 | 19 | (37) | 120 | 1,250 |
| Paul Quinn College* | 520 | (99.6) | 2 (0.4) | 522 | 1,849,506 | 627,138 | (33) | 37 | 0 | (0) | 95 | ND |
| Prairie View A&M University* | 4,749 | (85) | 845 (15) | 5,594 | 28,641,272 | 5,505,329 | (19) | 250 | 94 | (37) | 500 | ND |
| Rust College† | 800 | (100) | 0 (0) | 800 | 4,144,029 | 1,570,333 | (38) | 41 | 21 | (51) | 130 | 2,725 |
| Saint Augustine's College† | 1,529 | (100) | 0 (0) | 1,529 | 5,933,463 | 1,068,046 | (18) | 78 | 34 | (45) | 213 | 1,150 |

* Public
† Private
‡ No data; information not received.
Figures in parentheses represent percentages.

## UNIQUE FUNCTIONS OF BLACK COLLEGES

Black college presidents were asked in 1976 to tell us what their institutions do that is unique. These are some of the responses:

*Bennett College, Greensboro, North Carolina:* "Bennett College provides career-oriented education in a liberal arts context, primarily for black and other minority women . . . from a broad range of secondary school preparation and economic background."

*Delaware State College, Dover, Delaware:* "This college can and does succeed in reopening the doors which have been closed to so many students whose potentials have been judged by instruments developed for the majority culture."

*Elizabeth City State University, Elizabeth City, North Carolina:* "We pride ourselves in the Basic Education and Enrichment Program (BEEP) . . . which . . . gives supportive service to those students whose academic backgrounds reflect low levels of achievement . . . and which . . . provides an environment where any student can receive additional assistance in his respective field."

*Florida Agricultural and Mechanical University, Tallahassee, Florida:* "We . . . emphasize the academic programs offered in our School of Pharmacy and School of Architecture . . . not found in many of our predominantly Black institutions."

*Fort Valley State College, Fort Valley, Georgia:* "We have 'catch-up' academic programs for under-prepared freshmen."

*Huston-Tillotson College, Austin, Texas:* "We take the time necessary and provide the faculty required to reach students where they are when they come to College and help to prepare them for successful productive participation in an expanding American society."

*Knoxville College, Knoxville, Tennessee:* "Knoxville College takes significant numbers of students who have deficiencies and assists them in graduating, with competitive competencies."

*LeMoyne-Owen College, Memphis, Tennessee:* "We enroll students who are not typically thought of as college material and convert them in four years into people who can compete for jobs or in graduate or professional schools."

*Federal City College, Washington, DC:*[2] "FCC enrolls a large number of full-time and part-time students who have been out of the mainstream of formal education for 10 years or more; . . . many of our students are the first generation in their family to attend college."

[2]Since the study was conducted, this school has been renamed the University of the District of Columbia.

*Morgan State University, Baltimore, Maryland:* "Morgan has been geared for many years to develop, and improve, programs for instructing in the basic skills in mathematics, reading, writing, and speech."

*North Carolina Agricultural and Technical State University, Greensboro, North Carolina:* "North Carolina A&T State University provides an important opportunity for higher education for Blacks and other minorities who otherwise would be denied such an opportunity. The Black college or university president or chancellor, professor, department chairman, etc., are needed models of success that are achievable in the eyes of Black youth."

*Paine College, Augusta, Georgia:* "Paine College . . . is small enough to identify students in need and give them the kinds of inspiration and goading they need to maximize their potential. For a decade, Black institutions have taken students who might not be admitted to other institutions, and in four or five years have produced individuals who go on to graduate school and who make significant contributions to society."

*Paul Quinn College, Waco, Texas:* "There are few traditionally minority schools offering special curricula in the areas of undergraduate social work, medical technology, and recreational leadership. Paul Quinn College offers all three of these."

*Rust College, Holly Springs, Mississippi:* "I consider these programs unique at Rust College: The Freshmen Interdisciplinary program which develops self-concept and motivation for rapid achievement among students whose backgrounds are less than favorable; the Summer Study Skills program provided four weeks of intensive training for all new students prior to enrollment at Rust."

*St. Augustine's College, Raleigh, North Carolina:* "Some of the unique things that we do here at Saint Augustine's College are: The Talent Search Program and the Cooperative Education Program. The primary purpose of [the talent-search] program is to identify, counsel, and assist talented youth, who might have been overlooked by traditional means, to pursue post-secondary courses of study. The cooperative education program provides an opportunity for the students to actually get 'on the job' experience."

*Tuskegee Institute, Tuskegee, Alabama:* "Tuskegee is sensitive to the needs of the students we serve in the classroom and of the community we touch in many ways."

*University of Arkansas at Pine Bluff, Pine Bluff, Arkansas:* "The school has always used its resources to get an education for every student that could be reasonably brought within its fold. This included the underachiever, the penniless, and those who, based on standardized conceptions, could never make it."

## PRIORITIES FOR BLACK COLLEGES

Despite their unique educational programs, the contributions of Black colleges and universities to our national life have yet to be fully recognized. The belief that Black colleges should be abolished had been expressed covertly but was openly advocated by some in the 1970s. This threat has influenced the priorities of Black college presidents so that survival was the order of the day.

Committed to educating all who were willing to work diligently for a college education, presidents of Black colleges under siege still had to give attention to refurbishing or expanding the physical plant and to finding funds for buildings, student aid, faculty salaries, and other educational matters as well as justifying the existence of their schools. In our study, the median annual tuition in 1976 was $1,175 for the private Black college and $476 for the public Black college. Since the annual income of Blacks continues to be less than that of Whites at all income levels, increased tuition is not the most promising source of new revenue. The Black college presidents recognized this fact. They indicated that the fulfillment of approximately 35–40 percent of their priorities depend on resources external to their institutions.

The presidents listed eighty-one priorities for the future development of their schools, as seen in table 2.3. Some presidents mentioned as few as two priorities; others cited as many as eight. The average was four. About half of the priorities dealt with educational matters such as curriculum reform, faculty development, improving the system for advising students, innovations in career education including the design of new graduate programs, and undergraduate concentrations in the professions.

About one-third of the priorities had to do with finances, including capital improvements in the physical plant and increased funds for student aid, salaries for faculty and support staff, library acquisitions, and other academic needs. It should be noted that refurbishing or adding to the physical plant was not mentioned frequently as a priority. Most of the financial priorities had to do with student aid, faculty salaries, and basic operations.

**Table 2.3.   Priorities of fifteen presidents of Black colleges, 1976**

| Priorities | Number of Presidents | % of Total Priorities |
|---|---|---|
| Educational | 41 | 50 |
| Financial | 28 | 33 |
| Physical Plant (4) | | |
| Operating Funds (24) | | |
| Management | 12 | 17 |
| Totals | 81 | 100% |

## MANAGEMENT PRIORITIES

In the 1970s, foundations were interested in helping Black college administrators improve their management skills. As a consequence, workshops and institutes for business managers and other key officers were held. However, improvement in management procedures was infrequently mentioned by presidents in the survey; it was a priority for slightly more than one-sixth of the respondents. Among the management concerns of these presidents were the recruitment of students, public relations, long-range planning, establishment of an efficient decision-making process, improving the registration and record-keeping system, and developing a uniform pay scale for full-time employees. Presidents listed the recruitment of students as the most pressing matter.

### Recruitment of Students

The competition experienced by Black colleges from predominantly White schools for the enrollment of Black students is severe. In his response to our survey, Hugh Gloster, former president of Morehouse College, stated that the private Black colleges are handicapped in the competition because they have received no support to launch a similar campaign to attract White students: "In the South, White students attend predominantly Black colleges in significant numbers only if there are no predominantly White colleges in the community or if the predominantly Black colleges are public institutions with low tuition rates. We try to recruit White students but are unsuccessful. In a country where foundations and corporations have provided millions of dollars to predominantly White colleges to recruit Black students, we have sought funds to recruit White students but have been unsuccessful. As a matter of fact, I know of no predominantly Black college that has received a large grant providing scholarship money to attract White students" (Willie and MacLeish 1978, 142).

## EDUCATIONAL PRIORITIES: CLASSICAL VERSUS CAREER EDUCATION

The characteristic of Black institutions of higher education that have probably contributed most to their survival is their flexibility. They tend to change in accordance with requirements of the situation. The historic controversy between W. E. B. Du Bois and Booker T. Washington as to whether Black colleges should provide a liberal arts education or vocational training has been resolved and is not now an issue among Black college presidents. In the words of one administrator, her college "provides career-oriented education in a liberal arts context" (Willie and MacLeish 1978, 138).

In *Culture Out of Anarchy: The Reconstruction of American Higher Learning,* Judson Jerome told about Antioch's Inner College, with which he was affiliated at the time. One focus of activity at the Inner College for men and women students was "baking bread." Jerome noted approvingly that some young people in college had turned their attention to learning how to survive. Literally, their education was in the "hard subject of providing heat and food for themselves, making do with almost no . . . convenience." Such educational experiences had been fashioned, he said, because "young people have a genuine desire to rediscover their hands" (Jerome 1971, 266). The twentieth century was two-thirds spent before some colleges and universities recognized this desire in the young who came to them for an education.

Black educators recognized this desire decades earlier, at the beginning of this century. In 1903, Booker T. Washington said, "the very best service which any one can render to what is called the higher education is to teach the present generation to provide a material . . . foundation." Elaborating on this point, he said that "I have been discouraged as I have gone through the South . . . and have found [people] who could converse intelligently upon abstruse subjects, and yet could not tell how to improve the condition of the poorly cooked . . . bread . . . which they and their families were eating three times a day" (Washington 1970, 224). Washington called learning to work with one's hands industrial education. He defended it as a legitimate form of education that consists of teaching one "how to make the forces of nature . . . work for [one]." He concluded that if industrial education (that is, rediscovering one's hands and learning how to provide heat, food, and other essentials) has any value, "it is in lifting labor up out of toil and drudgery into the plane of the dignified and the beautiful" (225).

Jerome endorsed this pragmatic orientation and the search for relevance found among students in the 1960s. However, he looked to "liberal education [to] enlarge . . . a narrow pragmatic orientation toward education and human worth." Liberal education, he said, "has something to do with the definition of [men and women] with [their] unique awareness of [their] own mortality, [their] capacity for reflection, for holding the future and past along with the present in [their] mind[s]" (Jerome 1971, 275).

It took the student uprisings of the 1960s to bring Jerome and other educators to their senses about the multiple functions of liberal education to deal with the pragmatic as well as the philosophical, and the collective as well as the individual. Yet in 1903, W. E. B. Du Bois wrote that "it is the [person] and not the material product that is the true object of education" (1970, 227). He defined education as "that whole system of human training within and without school house walls, which molds and develops [people]" (226). Du Bois drew attention to the "street academy" and the "university without walls" decades before they were fashionable and faddish. The development of the mind, for him, was a continuous process not limited to any place or any age category.

Moreover, Du Bois saw moral education as an essential component of higher education: "Education must not simply teach work—it must teach life" (1970, 229). For Du Bois, education had the threefold function of strengthening character, increasing knowledge, and teaching one how to earn a living. Du Bois admitted that it was hard to do all of these simultaneously. But he said, resolutely, "It will not do to give all the attention to one and neglect the other" (226).

Had Jerome and other educators learned the wisdom of Du Bois, they would have recognized early on that pragmatic and philosophical orientations complement each other in higher education, that a dollar sign and a job can be one motivation for obtaining more schooling, and that learning how to promote justice can also be an objective of higher education.

Commenting upon the interrelationships among knowledge, character, and work, Du Bois said, "We might simply increase [one's] knowledge of the world, but this would not necessarily make one wish to use this knowledge honestly; we might seek to strengthen character and purpose, but to what end if . . . people have nothing to eat or to wear" (Du Bois 1970, 226).

Both Du Bois and Washington were influenced by their debate. Washington finally conceded that training of the hands without mental training as well is a crude kind of training for selfish purposes and is inappropriate (Washington 1970, 223). Du Bois admitted that the teaching of work is an important function of education. Indeed, he called it "the paramount necessity." But then he said, "Work alone will not do . . . unless inspired by the right ideals and guided by intelligence" (Du Bois 1970, 227–228). The essential difference between Booker T. Washington and W. E. B. Du Bois was not educational but political, involving strategy and tactics for race relations and social change. They wrestled with the idea of education and achieved a consensus that the pragmatic and the theoretical go hand in hand. Their understanding of higher education was ignored by other educators in the nation. It was during the 1960s that a learned professor would write: "If a college is to produce educated [people], it should concern itself with both liberal and practical education" (Jerome 1971, 264). Such an affirmation is based on the foundation of the Washington-Du Bois debate a half century earlier, which was not acknowledged as the intellectual heritage of a "new" understanding.

Why did it take the leaders of American higher education so long to deal with the issues raised in the Washington-Du Bois debate? The answer I derive is racism. White America ignored the Washington-Du Bois debate as two

Blacks fussing with each other, making "much ado about nothing." White America did not realize that the issues with which these men were wrestling were central to the education of all people. We must not commit this error again and ignore the initiatives of Black educators and Black schools. America has much to learn from the Black experience.

## ARCHETYPE OF AN EDUCATED PERSON

The life of Martin Luther King Jr. is a magnificent example of the purpose of education from the Black perspective in America. A decade after his death, Hugh Gloster of Morehouse College called King the "archetype of an educated person—one who combined academic achievement and professional success with personal integrity and social concern." He said that the life of Martin Luther King Jr. was worthy of emulation by all (Morehouse College 1980, 5).

The flexibility of Black colleges that has enabled them to combine the classical and the contemporary, including liberal arts and vocational skills, illustrates what can be done and how it may be accomplished. There are lessons in this synthesis for all institutions in higher education. Rather than looking backward, Black colleges have been in the vanguard. Indeed, the Du Bois-Washington debate dealt with a major issue in higher education in America but was not recognized as such because of the race of the participating parties.

Some of the new career options offered to Black college students in the 1970s were undergraduate concentrations in social work, medical technology, and recreational leadership. One president stated that his school had adopted a mandatory cooperative education program with a view toward using the world of work and its potential rewards to motivate and train students as well as provide earned income to lessen dependence on federal and state financial aid.

To summarize, the educational priorities of presidents of Black colleges in the 1970s were the initiation of cooperative education programs; changing the curriculum to include courses that lead to employment in a variety of vocations; the development of preprofessional programs in medicine and law; and providing a learning community that emphasized academic achievement, vocational success, personal integrity, and social concern.

## RACIAL COMPOSITION OF THE STUDENT BODY

In the light of the *Adams v. Richardson* decision of the Supreme Court in 1973, which required unitary state school systems for higher education, questions were frequently raised about the racial composition of the student body of Black colleges and universities. This study asked Black college presidents to respond to these questions: How do you feel about racial integration in higher education? Do you have non-Black students in your student body? If so, what is the size of your student body, and how many non-Blacks are on campus? Did they come on their own initiative, or did you recruit them?

Of the fifteen schools that responded, three recorded no Whites enrolled; for the twelve that had Whites, enrollments varied from 2 to 845 students. As mentioned earlier, Hugh Gloster responded that White students tend to enroll in public institutions with low tuitions. In our study, seven of the eight private institutions had a White student enrollment of fewer than 20 students. On the other hand, the state-supported predominantly Black schools had White students in their populations ranging from 200 to 845. The latter figure represented 15 percent of the total enrollment of Prairie View A&M University in Texas, the largest White enrollment in any of the southern schools participating in the study during the 1970s. The picture was quite different in some of the predominantly Black state colleges in the North, such as Delaware State; it had a 40 percent White enrollment.

Most predominantly Black schools indicated that their faculties are diversified and offer this fact to support the claim that they are racially open schools. The philosophy and policy of most predominantly Black schools is to accept students with disparate backgrounds. One president emphasized, however, that "government actions to reverse the consequences of centuries of racial desegregation must not be used as an excuse to dismantle or change the . . . orientation of the Black public colleges of the country" and their philosophy of education.

Black colleges are a classic illustration of being damned if you do and damned if you don't. For Black colleges and universities, antinomies appear to be eternal. These schools have a philosophy of what they would like to achieve. But they also are pragmatic and ingenious, and they know how to improvise. These are the sources of their salvation. It seems that some presidents a generation ago were rising to meet contemporary challenges as indicated by their priorities.

## AN APOLOGY FROM HARVARD

Presidents of Black colleges have been gravely offended by negative characterizations of their institutions, especially the one emanating from Harvard University. Stephen Wright, Benjamin Mays, Hugh Gloster, and Albert Dent gave spirited rejoinders to the Jencks-Riesman article (Wright et al. 1967, 451–467); but, in general, the administrators of many Black institutions of higher education suffered misunderstanding of their mission silently. First, the presidents of Black colleges were offended that Harvard academic colleagues with outstanding reputations would write such an article. Second, they were disappointed that a prestigious scholarly journal such as the *Harvard Educational Review* would consider the article to be a contribution to knowledge and worthy of publication.[3] Stephen Wright, former president of Fisk University, commenting on the Harvard connection of the professors who wrote the article and the periodical that published it, said that if it had not been "written by men of considerable reputation and published in a reputable journal, it would have . . . attracted little attention" (452).

In correspondence with the presidents of Black colleges during the course of this study, insight was gained into the depth of the distrust and hostility toward Harvard by some Black college leaders a generation ago. One Black college president said:

> I am writing in response to your letter . . . in which you refer to an earlier unanswered communication. Forgive my bad manners. I did not respond because I do not know the answers and am convinced that there are opinions [from other college presidents] which should not be watered down by any superficial comments from me.
>
> In addition, I am told that things which have come from your school in the past have been uncomplimentary to Black scholars and Black institutions. I am therefore afraid to be a part of your study. . . . Thanks for your understanding. (Willie and MacLeish 1978, 146)

Another put it this way:

> This is in response to your letter . . . requesting certain detailed information about our institution and for nominations to participate in your Conference.
>
> I regret that we will be unable to provide you with any information or to participate in your Conference.
>
> Those of us who work in the historically Black colleges feel that we have been studied enough, too often by persons who know least about these institutions and their contributions to American Higher Education and to the American society. The reports and writings flowing from these studies have been too often hyper and unfairly critical of our institutions, showing little sensitivity and even less understanding.
>
> You have my very best wishes for a meaningful and constructive endeavor. (Willie and MacLeish 1978, 146)

[3] As an indicator of changing practices over the years, in 1992 the *Harvard Educational Review* published "The Color of Success: African-American College Student Outcomes at Predominantly White and Historically Black Public Colleges and Universities," an article by Walter Allen that praised the pedagogical techniques of HBCUs (Allen 1992).

Still another Black college president refused to answer our inquiry until he had been assured by one of his faculty members, a recent graduate of the Harvard Graduate School of Education, that the principal investigator was Black. Having been abused once by Harvard researchers, many Black college presidents were reluctant to risk the possibility of a second coming without extraordinary reassurances.

The irony is that in the spring of 1967, the same year in which a Harvard-based publication announced to the world that Black colleges were "academic disaster areas" (Jencks and Riesman 1967, 26), Harvard University at its commencement awarded an honorary doctor of law degree to Benjamin Elijah Mays, the retiring president of Morehouse College, for his outstanding accomplishments as head of a Black college for nearly three decades;[4] 1967 was a banner year for Harvard in terms of the contradictory signals it gave out about Black education and the education of Blacks. A redeeming fact is that Harvard does not recoil from being contradictory.

It was in this tradition and spirit that the director of the Black College Conference of 1976 at Harvard apologized on behalf of the institution at the opening session for the distorted characterization of Black colleges published a decade earlier. No one at Harvard took exception to that apology or disassociated himself or herself from it. The apology, therefore, stood as stated. It should also be noted that during the Black College Conference, David Riesman disavowed his earlier position (Pressley 1976).

## JUDGING BLACK COLLEGES

The survey in 1976 revealed that Black college presidents will no longer suffer misunderstanding silently. Black colleges are not self-sufficient. They are as much dependent on others for their survival as any college or university in America. Despite their dependence (or maybe because of it), they have decided to fight back. Indeed, the 1976 study revealed that the administrators of Black institutions were in an aggressive mood.

They were poised to participate in the assessment of their schools and in defining their future. They insisted that Black colleges should be judged in terms of the way they fulfilled their unique mission and not by some measuring device that uses Harvard and other Ivy League schools as the standard.

---

[4]We also note that in the year 2003, Harvard University awarded an honorary doctorate degree to Norman Francis, president of Xavier University, a predominantly Black Catholic school in which a majority of matriculating students are Protestant or non-Catholic.

A generation ago, when many Black college presidents were fighting back, this is how they answered the question, "What else ought the nation know about Black colleges?" One college president said:

> The nation should know that the . . . Black colleges are and have been a critical national resource. They prepared the multi-culture in the nation. In the past 20 years, these colleges have produced a quarter of a million graduates and continue to turn out 30,000 graduates per year. Though more than 60 percent of Black college youth are enrolled in White colleges less than 40 percent of Black college youth graduate from White colleges. Black colleges have the expertise and climate conducive to all youth. They have had an open door policy for all ethnic groups for more than a century and have administered specifically to Black youth through these years. As a national asset, they need national support. (Willie and MacLeish 1978, 147)

Another declared:

> The nation ought to know that . . . the product of Black colleges, provide a unique, essential and priceless ingredient in American society that the nation can no longer do without nor afford to neglect. (Willie and MacLeish 1978, 148)

Still another put it this way:

> First of all, the nation must know that quality Black Colleges do exist on a level commensurate with (and in some areas higher than) comparable White institutions. It is incumbent upon Black Colleges to make themselves known by the quality of their leadership and the scholarship of their faculty. (Willie and MacLeish 1978, 148)

Finally, a Black college president made this statement about what the nation should know:

> The nation ought to know that all higher education institutions exist on a continuum ranging from excellent to terrible and that Black and White institutions alike are arrayed all along it. There is only one Harvard; there are many good, fair, mediocre, and bad schools. They all try to serve the same purpose. Black colleges have as much right to persevere in this as others. The numberless mediocre and incompetent White colleges go on and on; if their existence is threatened, the threat has a purely economic basis—no one says they must close because they are inferior institutions. Black colleges that are no worse and possibly better, on the other hand, are threatened with closing because they are inferior. Clearly, this is more than slander; it is rank discrimination and blatant racism. We who support Black higher education must fight it with all our power. (Willie and MacLeish 1978, 148)

The NAFEO offered the following information:

> During the past 10 years, some eighty-seven historically Black colleges have graduated more Black students with baccalaureate degrees than all of the other American higher education institutions combined. Therefore, educators need to look beyond the mere enrollment of Blacks in White schools and, specifically, at the number of Blacks who graduate. (Willie and MacLeish 1978, 148)

The Black college presidents in 1976 who marshaled sufficient faith to risk participating in one more study by a Harvard professor did so, the authors believe, because they trusted that the purpose of the survey was to help set the record straight. Specifically, one president said, "This letter is written from the valley to the mountain in the forlorn hope that communicating our aspirations will do us some good. We can only hope" (Willie and MacLeish 1978, 148).

The authors of this chapter said that they appreciated the assistance of all, were grateful for their trust, and hoped this study has not betrayed their trust. They tried to make an accurate assessment of the Black colleges and to be a reliable medium for the transmission of the message of Black college presidents.

*Part II*

# THE CONTEMPORARY CASE FOR HISTORICALLY BLACK COLLEGES AND UNIVERSITIES

# Chapter Three

# Carriers of the Diversity Mantra

Joseph Jewell states that historically Black colleges and universities have "produced a tradition of inclusion in higher education" that embrace and sustain "workable diverse educational environments" (Jewell 2002, 9). Xavier University in New Orleans, Louisiana, is a good example of these kinds of schools. Truly, it is a diverse educational environment. Xavier is the only Black Catholic institution of higher education in the United States; however, a majority of students enrolled are Protestant. More than half of its students pursue science and mathematics concentrations, but only about a third (36 percent) of the students in the class of 1995 were in the top 10 percent of their high school class, and the median score for mathematics on the Scholastic Aptitude Test (SAT) for this class was 464 in a range from 200 to 800 points (Mitchell 1993, 292). Although a majority of students scored below 500 in the mathematics section of the SAT, Xavier sends many African Americans to medical schools for graduate study. The specific fields of study for most Xavier undergraduates are pharmacy, biology, and business administration.

Xavier is able to provide an effective education for students with wide variations in precollege backgrounds because of "a small group of determined professors" (Mitchell 1993, 244). They have "designed a system combining introductory courses that build in remedial work with student tutoring and study groups." Moreover, there is "individual attention from faculty and out-

---

The data used in this analysis were obtained from table 222 (presented here as table 3.2) in the *Digest of Education Statistics, 2000*. The data were compiled from 1998 fall enrollments for all degree-granting HBCUs, and the table was prepared by the U.S. Department of Education, National Center for Educational Statistics, *Digest of Education Statistics, 2000* (Washington, DC: U.S. Government Printing Office, 2000), 260–261.

reach to budding high school [students] who manifest aptitudes for science" (294). One Black student marveled at the diversity in the student body and how he had learned at Xavier "to relate to a lot of different types of people" within his own racial group (395).

Two-thirds of the students at Xavier University come from Louisiana, and only half of those who enter as freshmen complete their course of study. Many students who do graduate attend fine medical schools located in the northern as well as the southern regions of the nation. Many of the medical schools that accept Xavier graduates are traditionally White institutions (TWIs).

Ellis Cose, whose book *Color-Blind* is subtitled *Seeing beyond Race in a Race-Obsessed World,* reported that the faculty at Xavier has learned that "ability . . . can be found in the most unlikely places. Even for those who start out with little confidence and mediocre grades, failure is not a foregone conclusion, for . . . it is possible to raise confidence, aspirations, and even test scores." Cose concludes that "along the way [Xavier] has become a Mecca of sorts for those who want to beat the odds" (Cose 1997, 53). The same can be said of students at other historically Black colleges and universities (HBCUs). We believe that extraordinary achievements have been attained by ordinary students in these settings because the schools in which they enroll start with them where they are and are not reluctant to offer remedial help whenever necessary.

This is the philosophy of education of Norman Francis, president of Xavier University. He said, "From the beginning, we always believed that every youngster could learn, that the mind was an unlimited facility, that if you gave the support, provided the environment and the teachers, young people would exceed even their own potential. Where others would say, 'they're not going to make it,' we say, 'we think they can.' And we give them a chance" (Norman Francis, qtd. in Cose 1997, 53).

Professor John Monro at Miles College in the late 1960s developed "a college program designed to deal with under-prepared students" (Monro 1978, 236). He called it his four-points program:

1. "[Keep] a close professional scrutiny of what each student brings to college in the way of skills, information, and attitudes."
2. "[Develop] a program of teaching and learning that deals directly and efficiently with the needs of students in a firm and supportive way."
3. "[Recruit] a competent dedicated faculty who are interested in teaching students rather than just teaching a subject."
4. "[Use] a management [system] that keeps close tabs on what is going on: How teachers and students are doing, what works well and what doesn't and what new developments in learning theory can help in the work." (Monro 1978, 236)

Monro is persuaded, and so are we, that any college can implement this program.

If, according to John Rawls, society should be "a fair system of cooperation" and "no one deserves his [or her] . . . starting place in [it]," all human societies are obligated to give compensating advantage to those of less fortune, because it is to the mutual advantage of all to do so (Rawls 2001, 27, 101, 76, 77).

By rescuing the perishing and caring for the fallen, Black colleges and universities are performing a just action for a well-ordered society. This is a necessary effort that many educational institutions have neglected to perform.

It is common practice for colleges and universities in the United States to tout the high average SAT scores of their first-year entering class and to gain eminence because of the large proportion of applicants rejected during the admissions process. According to *Barron's Profiles of American Colleges,* "college entrance examinations play . . . an important role deciding who is admitted and who is rejected." Further, Barron reports that "poor results on these examinations may make it difficult for a student to gain acceptance to college, in spite of a relatively good high school record" (BES 1994, 8).

However, *The Multicultural Student's Guide to Colleges* prepared by Robert Mitchell found that many of America's premier colleges and universities now wish to serve "a broader spectrum of students and to have their student populations reflect more accurately the country's socioeconomic, racial and cultural diversity." Mitchell states that "increased recruiting and retention efforts" are needed to achieve these goals. Some schools are successfully changing their recruitment and retention practices. However, this is not yet true for all of the country's top schools (Mitchell 1993, 3).

It should be obvious (but apparently is not) that HBCUs could be of assistance to all higher education institutions that wish to diversify their student bodies. Joseph Jewell states that "HBCUs have long been a haven for those whose academic talents were unwelcome elsewhere" (Jewell 2002, 9). And according to Monro, "our major colleges and universities are losing out on a large number of able students because . . . [they] do not know how to find them or work with them" (Monro 1978, 236). These statements suggest that all colleges and universities have not made a full commitment to educate all students who wish to learn.

We repeat a few comments mentioned in chapter 2 by the presidents of several Black colleges and universities. These comments have to do with their students and the courses of study available to them (Willie and MacLeish 1978, 132–148). One said, "This college can and does succeed in reopening the doors which have been closed to so many students whose potentials have been judged by instruments developed for the majority culture." Another president said, "We take the time necessary and provide the faculty required to reach students where they are when they come to college and help to prepare them for successful productive participation in an expanding American society." Finally, a third president said, "We enroll students who are not typically thought of as college material and convert them in four years into people who can compete for jobs and graduate or professional schools" (138–139).

Morehouse College has a reputation for sending many of its students to graduate school even though a majority of Morehouse students were not among the "talented tenth" in their high school senior class. Nevertheless, a 1992 edition of *U.S. News and World Report* ranked it as "one of the best regional liberal arts colleges in the South" (Mitchell 1993, 187). About four out of every ten Morehouse College graduates matriculate in graduate school immediately after receiving a bachelor's degree. How a school, in which a majority of its students scored below 500 on the verbal section of the SAT, maintains high expectations and manages to achieve them for its students *is no secret.* It would be beneficial if other schools learned how to educate well students who may not be classified as the best and brightest. Morehouse students, in recent years, have begun to compete effectively for Rhodes scholarships. Through the year 2004, Morehouse has produced three Rhodes scholars, a number that is greater than any other Black college in the United States.

In addition to accommodating diversified student bodies of scholars with a variety of aptitudes and learning styles, HBCUs aspire to be racially diversified learning communities. This they have done with reference to faculty and their racial characteristics, and also with students who have a variety of learning styles and socioeconomic backgrounds; however, these schools have some distance to go to achieve an acceptable level of racial diversity among matriculating students.

As seen in table 3.1, there are about one-quarter of a million (248,931) students enrolled in historically Black colleges and universities that award four-year college degrees; they represent 3 percent of the more than 9.5 million students enrolled in higher education institutions who are studying for baccalaureate degrees (U.S. Department of Education 2000a, 245). In all degree-granting HBCUs, Black students are a majority (82 percent) in combined public and private student bodies, and students other than Blacks are a minority (18 percent), as seen in table 3.2. A higher portion of all students in HBCUs—70 percent—enroll in publicly supported schools, and only 30 percent attend private schools. Data reported above are for the year 1998.

We stated earlier that HBCUs have some distance to go to achieve an acceptable level of racial diversity in student enrollment. Social science studies have found that a minimum critical mass of 20 percent of the student body consist-

Table 3.1.   Enrollment in four-year public and private historically Black colleges and unversities, United States, 1998

| Type of College or University | Black Men | Black Women | Total Black | Total Other | Total All | % of Black Students | % of Other Students | Total |
|---|---|---|---|---|---|---|---|---|
| Public | 55,970 | 87,015 | 142,985 | 31,791 | 174,776 | 82 | 18 | 100 |
| Private | 27,026 | 41,811 | 68,837 | 5,318 | 74,155 | 93 | 7 | 100 |
| Total | 82,996 | 128,826 | 211,822 | 37,109 | 248,931 | 85 | 15 | 100 |

*Note:* Historically Black colleges and universities are degree-granting institutions established prior to 1964.
*Source:* U.S. Department of Education, National Center for Education Statistics, General Information
   Survey, *Digest of Educational Statistics, 2000* (Washington, DC: U.S. Government Printing Office, 2000),
   262.

Table 3.2.   Percent fall enrollment and degrees conferred in degree-granting historically Black colleges by institutions, 1998

| Total Enrollment, Fall 1998 | Number | Percent |
|---|---|---|
| Black | 223,745 | 81.8 |
| Non-Black | 49,727 | 18.2 |
| Total | 273,472 | 100 |

| Degrees Conferred, 1997–1998 | Number | Percent |
|---|---|---|
| Associate | 3,407 | 8.2 |
| Bachelor's | 29,780 | 72 |
| Master's | 6,411 | 15.5 |
| Doctorate | 377 | 1 |
| First professional degree | 1,348 | 3.3 |
| Total | 41,323 | 100 |

*Source:* U.S. Department of Education, National Center for Education Statistics, Higher Education General
   Information Survey (HEGIS), "Fall Enrollment in Institutions of Higher Education"; and Integrated
   Postsecondary Education Data System (IPEDS), "Fall Enrollment," "Completions," and "Finance" surveys.
   The table was prepared by the U.S. Department of Education, National Center for Education Statistics,
   *Digest of Education Statistics, 2000* (Washington, DC: U.S. Government Printing Office, 2000), 260–262.
   This table included data from two-year and four-year colleges.

ing of a single minority group or a combination of several minority groups is necessary for the minority component of a school community to have a meaningful impact on the total institution. Student groups other than the majority Black population in HBCUs are about one-sixth of HBCU student bodies as a collectivity. This means that they are 2 percentage points below the minimum proportion. Public HBCUs have minority populations that are closer to the minimum critical mass of non-Black students than private HBCUs. Only 7 percent of the students in private HBCUs are members of a racial group other than Black, while the proportion of non-Black students in public HBCUs is more than twice the proportion of such students in private HBCUs.

Research studies have found that when the members of identifiable sub-dominant groups (singly or combined) are less than one out of every five students, their opinions are seldom taken into consideration in community decision making by the dominant group. Also, studies have found that minority groups that are smaller than the critical mass of 20 percent of a school community's population tend to experience a sense of isolation within the learning environment, as well as estrangement between members of their own group (Willie 1978, 68).

Using 1998 data, we found that non-Black students are 2 percent or less in some HBCUs. This is true in a few well-known private HBCUs such as Talladega College, Clark Atlanta University, Morehouse College, Spelman College, Dillard University, Tougaloo College, Johnson C. Smith University, Fisk University, and Virginia Union University.

As mentioned earlier, Hugh Gloster, former president of Morehouse College, explained that so few non-Black students are enrolled in these and other private HBCUs because their tuitions are relative high compared to tuition in public HBCUs. Thus, according to Gloster, non-Black students tend to enroll in public HBCUs that have lower tuitions (Willie and MacLeish 1978, 44), bypassing private HBCUs that are members of the United Negro College Fund (UNCF).

Treating Gloster's statement as a hypothesis, we examined the enrollment of all UNCF schools (using 1998 data) and discovered that only 4 percent of students in all of these schools combined classified themselves as members of a racial group other than Black. A few schools varied from this average—schools such as Huston-Tillotson College (24 percent of students are non-Black), Florida Memorial College (17 percent of students are non-Black), and Oakwood College (16 percent of students are non-Black), as reported in table 3.3 (U.S. Department of Education 2000, 260–261). Thus, a few private HBCUs had diversity scores that are similar to or greater than the average diversity score for all public HBCUs, although the tuition charges in these three private schools were higher than those in most public HBCUs. These schools should be carefully studied to determine their cross-racial attraction.

In 1998, the average tuition in public, land-grant HBCUs was between $2,000 and $3,000, while the average tuition in private HBCUs was between $7,000 and $8,000. The relatively low enrollment of White and Brown students in most private HBCUs tends to give some credibility to the Gloster hypothesis, mentioned in chapter 2.

Deviations from the norm have been observed for some publicly supported HBCUs, too. An analysis of land-grant HBCUs in the eleven states in which UNCF schools also exist revealed that a few public HBCUs had non-Black student populations that were the same as or less than the low diversity score of 7 percent of non-Black students for all private HBCUs. Among the less diversified land-grant HBCUs were the University of Arkansas at Pine Bluff

(7 percent non-Black students), South Carolina State University (7 percent non-Black students), Southern University at Baton Rouge (6 percent non-Black students), and Alcorn State University in Mississippi (4 percent non-Black students). These public HBCUs with fewer non-Black students than other public institutions had low tuitions ranging from $2,646 to $2,974 and thus challenge in a partial way the Gloster hypothesis.

In opposition to the low-diversity public schools mentioned above, Alabama A&M University and Tennessee State University have as many as 19 percent to 27 percent non-Black students, respectively. The questions is, how can some public HBCUs attract nearly one-fifth or more of students who are different from the prevailing race of matriculating students while others do not?

While there seems to be partial support for the Gloster hypothesis, deviations from the norm by some private HBCUs that had non-Black minority student populations similar to or larger than the average for all public colleges and deviations from the public school norm by schools with only a few Whites are challenges to his hypothesis.

These findings suggest that phenomena other than tuition also affect the size of the non-Black student population in both public and private HBCUs. We arrived at this conclusion about the impact of other factors on the relative distribution of Black and non-Black students in public and private HBCUs after determining that among private HBCUs, a range of 24 percentage points exists between, for example, Benedict College and Lane College, with 100 percent Black student bodies, and Huston-Tillotson College, in which 76 percent of the student population was Black in 1998. There was a similar range of 23 percentage points between land-grant public HBCUs with the highest and lowest proportion of Black students; in 1998, 96 percent of the students in Alcorn State University were Black, while 73 percent of the students in Tennessee State University were Black, according to the *Digest of Education Statistics* (U.S. Department of Education 2002a, 260–261). We need careful analyses of tuition costs, enrollment policies, school administration practices, school culture, and student preferences to arrive at sound conclusions about why some HBCUs are more diversified than others.

Although some of the best-known HBCUs have student bodies of which only 2 percent are White or non-Black, leaders of HBCUs have always contended that their schools may have been segregated but that they never were segregating institutions.

Benjamin Mays of Morehouse sincerely believed in integration. During the civil rights movement, he encouraged Hamilton Holmes, an honors student, to leave Morehouse and, with Charlayne Hunter, enroll in the University of Georgia to desegregate the state's top public university. Holmes did what he was encouraged to do and was elected to Phi Beta Kappa when he graduated.

Table 3.3.  Fall enrollment, degrees conferred, and expenditures in degree-granting historically Black colleges and universities, by institution, 1998

| 1 | 2 | Enrollment, 1998 | | Degrees conferred, 1997–98 | | | | | 10 | 11 |
|---|---|---|---|---|---|---|---|---|---|---|
| Institution | Type and control[1] | Total | Black | Associate | Bachelor's | Master's | Doctor's | First-professional | Current-fund expenditures for public institutions, 1996–97, in thousands | Total expenditures for private institutions, 1996–97, in thousands |
| 1 | 2 | 3 | 4 | 5 | 6 | 7 | 8 | 9 | 10 | 11 |
| Total | — | 273,472 | 223,745 | 3,407 | 29,780 | 6,411 | 377 | 1,348 | $2,234,791 | $1,527,421 |
| **Alabama A&M University, AL | 1 | 5,128 | 4,155 | — | 544 | 361 | 9 | — | 69,309 | — |
| Alabama State University, AL | 1 | 5,552 | 4,952 | 1 | 538 | 162 | — | — | 55,912 | — |
| Bishop State Community College, AL | 2 | 3,660 | 2,178 | 451 | — | — | — | — | 21,038 | — |
| C. A. Fredd State Technical College, AL | 2 | 225 | 99 | 1 | — | — | — | — | — | — |
| Concordia College, AL | 3 | 564 | 499 | 28 | 9 | — | — | — | — | 4,311 |
| Gadsden State Community College[2] | 2 | 4,651 | 869 | 555 | — | — | — | — | — | — |
| J. F. Drake Technical College, AL | 2 | 663 | 323 | 60 | — | — | — | — | 4,496 | — |
| Lawson State Community College, AL | 2 | 1,395 | 1,378 | 192 | — | — | — | — | 11,176 | — |
| Miles College, AL | 3 | 1,390 | 1,386 | — | 176 | — | — | — | — | 13,617 |
| Oakwood College, AL | 3 | 1,805 | 1,515 | 56 | 221 | — | — | — | — | 25,312 |
| Stillman College, AL | 3 | 1,017 | 976 | — | 187 | — | — | — | — | 16,644 |
| Talladega College, AL | 3 | 616 | 602 | — | 134 | — | — | — | — | 15,340 |
| Trenholm State Technical College, AL | 2 | 593 | 465 | 80 | — | — | — | — | 7,620 | — |
| **Tuskegee University, AL | 3 | 3,080 | 2,913 | — | 416 | 45 | — | 56 | — | 29,616 |
| Arkansas Baptist College, AR | 3 | 225 | 223 | — | 28 | — | — | — | — | 1,758 |
| Philander Smith College, AR | 3 | 921 | 881 | — | 95 | — | — | — | — | 8,327 |
| **University of Arkansas, Pine Bluff, AR | 1 | 3,069 | 2,865 | 1 | 370 | 9 | — | — | 37,042 | — |

| Institution | | | | | | | | | | |
|---|---|---|---|---|---|---|---|---|---|---|
| **Delaware State University, DE | 1 | 3,156 | 2,322 | — | 434 | 101 | — | — | 47,732 | — |
| Howard University, DC | 3 | 10,211 | 8,519 | — | 1,321 | 482 | 95 | 393 | — | 569,028 |
| **University of the District of Columbia, DC | 1 | 5,252 | 4,317 | 162 | 450 | 77 | — | — | 103,858 | — |
| University of the District of Columbia Law School, DC[3] | 1 | 158 | 103 | — | — | — | — | 60 | 3,575 | — |
| Bethune-Cookman College, FL | 3 | 2,481 | 2,278 | — | 273 | — | — | — | | 28,062 |
| Edward Waters College, FL | 3 | 704 | 670 | — | 31 | — | — | — | | 7,901 |
| **Florida A&M University, FL | 1 | 11,828 | 10,748 | 58 | 1,352 | 277 | 1 | 57 | 180,911 | — |
| Florida Memorial College, FL | 3 | 1,771 | 1,581 | — | 182 | — | — | — | | 16,487 |
| Albany State College, GA | 1 | 3,200 | 2,921 | — | 380 | 109 | — | — | 32,895 | — |
| Clark Atlanta University, GA | 3 | 5,410 | 5,300 | — | 591 | 385 | 46 | — | | 56,349 |
| **Fort Valley State College, GA | 1 | 2,685 | 2,476 | 5 | 282 | 142 | — | — | 38,989 | — |
| Interdenominational Theological Center, GA | 3 | 423 | 393 | — | — | 8 | 8 | 67 | | 5,965 |
| Morehouse College, GA | 3 | 3,148 | 3,142 | — | 515 | — | — | — | | 49,118 |
| Morehouse School of Medicine, GA | 3 | 178 | 142 | — | — | 7 | 2 | 36 | | 67,492 |
| Morris Brown College, GA | 3 | 2,013 | 1,973 | — | 139 | — | — | — | | 19,399 |
| Paine College, GA | 3 | 863 | 836 | — | 111 | — | — | — | | 8,391 |
| Savannah State College, GA | 1 | 2,288 | 2,092 | 3 | 314 | 32 | — | — | 30,805 | — |
| Spelman College, GA | 3 | 1,897 | 1,861 | — | 442 | — | — | — | | 43,641 |
| **Kentucky State University, KY | 1 | 2,302 | 1,276 | 92 | 226 | 25 | — | — | 38,440 | — |
| Dillard University, LA | 3 | 1,698 | 1,685 | — | 297 | — | — | — | | 23,465 |
| Grambling State University, LA | 1 | 5,162 | 4,916 | 47 | 875 | 114 | 10 | — | 63,725 | — |
| **Southern University and A&M College, Baton Rouge, LA | 1 | 9,572 | 9,040 | 41 | 1,078 | 248 | 2 | 103 | 99,694 | — |
| Southern University, New Orleans, LA | 1 | 4,113 | 3,824 | 19 | 480 | 115 | — | — | 24,029 | — |

**Table 3.3. Fall enrollment, degrees conferred, and expenditures in degree-granting historically Black colleges and universities, by institution, 1998**

| Institution | Type and control[1] | Enrollment, 1998 Total | Enrollment, 1998 Black | Associate | Bachelor's | Master's | Doctor's | First-professional | Current-fund expenditures for public institutions, 1996–97, in thousands | Total expenditures for private institutions, 1996–97, in thousands |
|---|---|---|---|---|---|---|---|---|---|---|
| 1 | 2 | 3 | 4 | 5 | 6 | 7 | 8 | 9 | 10 | 11 |
| Southern University, Shreveport-Bossier City Campus, LA | 2 | 1,399 | 1,281 | 128 | — | — | — | — | 8,298 | — |
| Xavier University of Louisiana, LA | 3 | 3,655 | 3,301 | — | 425 | 85 | — | 148 | — | 57,652 |
| Bowie State University, MD | 1 | 5,024 | 3,915 | — | 508 | 501 | — | — | 38,079 | — |
| Coppin State College, MD | 1 | 3,764 | 3,564 | — | 339 | 107 | — | — | 30,237 | — |
| Morgan State University, MD | 1 | 6,141 | 5,846 | — | 694 | 64 | 4 | — | 85,471 | — |
| **University of Maryland, Eastern Shore, MD | 1 | 3,206 | 2,359 | — | 415 | 73 | 3 | — | 44,309 | — |
| Lewis College of Business, MI | 4 | 308 | 270 | 21 | — | — | — | — | — | 1,259 |
| **Alcorn State University, MS | 1 | 2,860 | 2,732 | 18 | 430 | 114 | — | — | 44,044 | — |
| Coahoma Community College, MS | 2 | 1,086 | 1,056 | 87 | — | — | — | — | 9,345 | — |
| Hinds Community College, Utica Campus, MS | 2 | 1,118 | 1,051 | 65 | — | — | — | — | — | — |
| Jackson State University, MS | 1 | 6,292 | 5,901 | — | 629 | 289 | 29 | — | 70,826 | — |
| Mary Holmes College, MS | 4 | 406 | 394 | 37 | — | — | — | — | — | 5,773 |
| Mississippi Valley State University, MS | 1 | 2,448 | 2,309 | — | 285 | 20 | — | — | 27,026 | — |
| Rust College, MS | 3 | 852 | 809 | 6 | 129 | — | — | — | — | 12,983 |
| Tougaloo College, MS | 3 | 890 | 889 | — | 132 | — | — | — | — | 14,150 |

Degrees conferred, 1997–98 columns: Associate, Bachelor's, Master's, Doctor's, First-professional

| | | | | | | | | | | |
|---|---|---|---|---|---|---|---|---|---|---|
| Harris-Stowe State College, MO | 1 | 1,735 | 1,257 | — | 169 | — | — | — | 12,776 | — |
| **Lincoln University, MO | 1 | 3,214 | 882 | 75 | 337 | 90 | — | — | 31,740 | — |
| Barber-Scotia College, NC | 3 | 488 | 478 | — | 53 | — | — | — | — | 8,368 |
| Bennett College, NC | 3 | 603 | 590 | — | 89 | — | — | — | — | 5,613 |
| Elizabeth City State University, NC | 1 | 1,932 | 1,453 | — | 359 | — | — | — | 32,954 | — |
| Fayetteville State University, NC | 1 | 4,373 | 3,041 | 37 | 599 | 110 | 4 | — | 44,003 | — |
| Johnson C. Smith University, NC | 3 | 1,443 | 1,432 | — | 201 | 1 | — | — | — | 27,570 |
| Livingstone College, NC | 3 | 944 | 903 | — | 100 | — | — | 9 | — | 13,439 |
| **North Carolina Agricultural and Technical State University, NC | 1 | 7,465 | 6,583 | — | 1,036 | 253 | 2 | — | 115,068 | — |
| North Carolina Central University, NC | 1 | 5,743 | 4,705 | — | 741 | 236 | — | 95 | 68,605 | — |
| St. Augustine's College, NC | 3 | 1,598 | 1,443 | — | 130 | — | — | — | — | 22,849 |
| Shaw University, NC | 3 | 2,569 | 2,473 | 13 | 421 | — | — | — | — | 29,755 |
| Winston-Salem State University, NC | 1 | 2,889 | 2,299 | — | 502 | — | — | — | 40,405 | — |
| Central State University, OH | 1 | 1,026 | 951 | — | 252 | 5 | — | — | 36,553 | — |
| Wilberforce University, OH | 3 | 963 | 887 | — | 211 | — | — | — | — | 13,906 |
| **Langston University, OK | 1 | 3,235 | 2,094 | — | 488 | 10 | — | — | 29,243 | — |
| Cheyney University of Pennsylvania, PA | 1 | 1,742 | 1,577 | — | 177 | 93 | — | — | 24,854 | — |
| Lincoln University, PA | 1 | 2,084 | 1,898 | — | 185 | 133 | — | — | 32,755 | — |
| Allen University, SC | 3 | 359 | 352 | — | 23 | — | — | — | — | 3,325 |
| Benedict College, SC | 3 | 2,405 | 2,405 | — | 193 | — | — | — | — | 18,743 |
| Claflin College, SC | 3 | 1,161 | 1,130 | — | 140 | — | — | — | — | 13,864 |
| Denmark Technical College, SC | 2 | 1,189 | 1,085 | 84 | — | — | — | — | 5,675 | — |
| Morris College, SC | 3 | 888 | 884 | — | 138 | — | — | — | — | 12,094 |
| **South Carolina State University, SC | 1 | 4,795 | 4,444 | — | 563 | 216 | 24 | — | 60,481 | — |
| Voorhees College, SC | 3 | 966 | 941 | — | 152 | — | — | — | — | 12,210 |

Table 3.3. Fall enrollment, degrees conferred, and expenditures in degree-granting historically Black colleges and universities, by institution, 1998

| Institution | Type and control[1] | Enrollment, 1998 | | Degrees conferred, 1997–98 | | | | | Current-fund expenditures for public institutions, 1996–97, in thousands | Total expenditures for private institutions, 1996–97, in thousands |
| | | Total | Black | Associate | Bachelor's | Master's | Doctor's | First-professional | | |
| 1 | 2 | 3 | 4 | 5 | 6 | 7 | 8 | 9 | 10 | 11 |
| Fisk University, TN | 3 | 826 | 809 | — | 129 | 12 | — | — | — | 8,219 |
| Lane College, TN | 3 | 626 | 626 | — | 86 | — | — | — | — | 9,730 |
| LeMoyne-Owen College, TN | 3 | 846 | 829 | — | 136 | 2 | — | — | — | 10,804 |
| Meharry Medical College, TN | 3 | 856 | 637 | — | — | 23 | 16 | 148 | — | 70,864 |
| ***Tennessee State University, TN | 1 | 8,750 | 6,401 | 90 | 822 | 325 | 35 | — | 87,595 | — |
| Huston-Tillotson College, TX | 3 | 618 | 469 | — | 69 | — | — | — | — | 9,444 |
| Jarvis Christian College, TX | 3 | 500 | 473 | — | 35 | — | — | — | — | 8,465 |
| Paul Quinn College, TX | 3 | 742 | 664 | — | 95 | — | — | — | — | 8,891 |
| **Prairie View A&M University, TX | 1 | 5,996 | 5,233 | — | 720 | 379 | — | — | 74,517 | — |
| St. Philip's College, TX | 2 | 7,848 | 164 | 395 | 2 | — | — | — | 30,529 | — |
| Southwestern Christian College, TX | 3 | 186 | 1,474 | 28 | 16 | — | — | — | — | 3,850 |
| Texas College, TX | 3 | 261 | 258 | — | 16 | — | — | — | — | — |
| Texas Southern University, TX | 1 | 6,316 | 5,275 | — | 671 | 106 | 16 | 176 | 70,808 | — |
| Wiley College, TX | 3 | 662 | 570 | — | 104 | — | — | — | — | 9,318 |

| Institution | | | | | | | | | |
|---|---|---|---|---|---|---|---|---|---|
| Hampton University, VA | 3 | 5,635 | 4,904 | 23 | 830 | 100 | 3 | — | 77,056 |
| Norfolk State University, VA | 1 | 7,115 | 6,154 | 45 | 881 | 199 | 3 | 76,059 | — |
| St. Paul's College, VA | 3 | 602 | 578 | — | 141 | — | — | — | 9,773 |
| **Virginia State University, VA | 1 | 4,341 | 3,883 | — | 430 | 133 | — | 53,493 | — |
| Virginia Union University, VA | 3 | 1,596 | 1,564 | — | 142 | — | 65 | — | 17,230 |
| Bluefield State College, WV | 1 | 2,405 | 201 | 173 | 225 | — | — | — | 14,674 |
| West Virginia State College, WV | 1 | 4,817 | 613 | 197 | 358 | — | — | — | 27,974 |
| **University of the Virgin Islands, St. Thomas Campus, VI | 1 | 1,603 | 1,408 | 33 | 152 | 33 | — | — | 35,149 |

— Not available.
** Land-grant institution.
[1] 1=public 4-year; 2=public 2-year; 3=private 4-year; and 4=private 2-year.
[2] In 1998, school became a historically Black college. School opened in 1960 as Gadsden Vocational Trade School, a private training facility.
[3] Was formerly included in the University of the District of Columbia. In 1997, it was reported separately.
*Note:* Historically Black colleges and universities that are not Title IV participating are not in this table. Schools that are not Title IV participating are not eligible for student financial aid.

*Source:* U.S. Department of Education, National Center for Education Statistics, Integrated Postsecondary Education Data System (IPEDS), "Fall Enrollment, 1998," "Completions, 1997–98," and "Finance, 1996–97" surveys. (This table was prepared August 2000.)

Hunter graduated also and returned to the campus of the University of Georgia a quarter of a century later to deliver the commencement address.

In 1994, Morehouse accepted a White student named Steven Schukei from Nebraska (discussed in greater detail in chapter 4) and nurtured him so effectively that he became deeply involved in campus political activity and was elected vice president of student government his senior year. Despite this good experience, the number of matriculating White students in most private Black colleges and universities has remained very low. Apparently, special recruitment efforts are needed to further integrate HBCUs so that White students can enjoy the benefit of being a minority in an institution where the dominant group consists of Black people.

John Jackson's dissertation presented to Harvard University to fulfill requirements for his Doctor of Education degree in 2001 analyzed North Carolina's plan designed to desegregate all schools in the state system of higher education. Ninety-five percent of White students who attended public HBCUs in North Carolina came because they received financial aid; 66 percent received full tuition grants. Focus group discussions revealed that "low tuition" of public HBCUs, "receiving a scholarship," and "financial factors" were most frequently mentioned by White students as reasons for attending a state-supported HBCU. Of the six schools Jackson studied (three HBCUs and three TWIs), the TWIs had nine Black members on the admissions staff with responsibility for recruiting Black students; but the HBCUs had only three White individuals on the admissions staff dedicated to recruiting White students. The TWIs engaged Black students to help recruit other Black students, but the HBCUs seldom turned to White students enrolled to help recruit other White students (Jackson 2001, 80, 81, 91, 92).

Finally, Jackson found that TWIs had sessions targeted to Black students and invited them to visit the campus as a recruitment strategy, but that HBCUs "rarely . . . bring prospective White students to the campus" before they enrolled. Black students in TWIs found the Office of Minority Affairs "a place that serves as a tremendous support . . . on campus." However, HBCUs seldom had a minority affairs office to support White students as the minority on their campuses (Jackson 2001, 96, 103).

These findings pertaining to the North Carolina plan for desegregating public higher education, and especially the finding that "financial aid was . . . the most essential factor in recruiting Whites to HBCUs" (Jackson 2001, 102), indicate that deliberate efforts to help White students with limited income may demonstrably enhance racial diversity on the campus of Black colleges and universities.

To the extent that the higher cost of an education in private HBCUs is an impediment to achieving a diversified student body, we urge the great foundations of this nation to do for historically Black colleges and universities today what was done for traditionally White educational institutions in the 1960s, as mentioned in chapter 2. The Rockefeller Foundation, for example, launched a new program that gave primary attention "to ways to improve higher education opportunities for disadvantaged minorities." The foundation believed that "the soundest way to accomplish this was to help open the door of good universities to minority group candidates" (Rockefeller Foundation 1968, 116).

In September 1964, the first recruits enrolled in such universities as Duke, Emory, Tulane, and Vanderbilt. Institutions such as Antioch, Carleton, Grinnell, Oberlin, Occidental, Reed, and Swarthmore . . . were characterized by the Foundation as "strong liberal arts colleges"[.] [They] received grants in 1964 and 1965 to recruit more minority students. By 1966 and 1967 this program had extended to Bowdoin, Brooklyn College of the City University of New York, Claremont, Cornell, and the University of California at Los Angeles. Annual expansion of the program was possible because knowledge had been gained from three Foundation-sponsored pilot programs for identifying promising minority students. These pilot programs were undertaken at Princeton, Dartmouth and Oberlin as early as 1963. (Willie 1991, 9–10)

Given that foundation-sponsored scholarship assistance helped to integrate Black students into White colleges in the 1960s and during the closing decades of the twentieth century, there is reason to believe that foundation-sponsored scholarships will help integrate White students into predominantly Black colleges and universities in the early decades of the twenty-first century.

We know that HBCUs have developed useful pedagogical methods that have helped students overcome difficulties of the past and go on to be successful members of society. There are numerous White students who need the care and concern that HBCUs, and particularly private HBCUs, lavish on their students. These students should not be denied such because private HBCUs may be more expensive than publicly supported schools. The same case that was made for diversifying predominantly White colleges and universities in the 1960s can be made for HBCUs today. Both kinds of school need diversified student bodies—an educational asset.

The few non-Black students who enroll in HBCUs have received some important educational benefits, such as knowledge that Black schools provide a good education, that teachers in these schools help all students and are not partial because of the race of a student, and that courses offered by these school contribute to obtaining good jobs in the future (Willie 1981a, 82).

The White students enrolled in HBCUs also reported that they saw themselves in a different way and that they dismissed old racial stereotypes from their thinking. Actually, 75–80 percent said their education on Black campuses heightened their appreciation of different ways of life and caused them to be more concerned about equal opportunity for all. Moreover, they felt that their multicultural experience would help them to be more effective in their careers (Willie 1981a, 89–90). This information was obtained from a reanalysis by Charles Willie (1981a) of a survey of Whites in predominantly Black colleges and universities conducted in the 1970s by Nancy V. Standley (1978).

As the great foundations and public service organizations in the latter third of the twentieth century were concerned about bringing young Black people into the mainstream through the integration of traditionally White institutions, so should they be concerned about developing genuine empathy on the part of young White people for individuals unlike themselves by assisting them to attend and integrate HBCUs. Interracial empathy can be developed effectively among White students who integrate historically Black colleges as minority students and among Blacks who integrate TWIs. Empathy can be developed only by direct and continuous participation in the way of life of others (Buber 1955, 107). And this is what integration of Whites with people of color in HBCUs could achieve.

Empathy most easily develops among subdominant people of power, minorities, and people who are not in charge. Sociologist Robert Merton recognized the value of minority status several years ago when he said, "It is not infrequently the case that the non-conforming minority in society represents the interest and ultimate values of the group more effectively than the conforming 'majority'" (Merton 1968, 421).

Few school desegregation plans assign Whites to schools in which they will be minorities. A Richmond, Virginia, school official told one of the authors why this seldom occurs. He said, "The White middle-class will not submerge [its] values to those of an antithetical culture" and the "White middle class America will accept a 15 to 20 percent Black population in [the White] child's school if [the Blacks] are middle class" (qtd. in Willie 1981a, 79). This attitude by a school district central administrator forecloses the opportunity for Whites to benefit from the opportunity and privilege of being a minority.

In a national society and global world in which the proportion of people of color is increasing and the proportion of White people is decreasing, it is meet and right to prepare Whites to gracefully accept minority status and to be creatively fulfilled in carrying out minority role responsibilities. HBCUs can play an important role in this transformation of society due to demographic changes by gracefully accepting White students into HBCUs as full-fledged members of the college or university with all rights and responsibilities appertaining thereto. Just as integrating Black students into TWIs had a beneficial educational outcome, we believe the integration of White and Brown students into HBCUs will have a beneficial outcome.

John Monro, a White educator who resigned from his position as dean of Harvard College in 1967, joined the faculty of Miles College in Alabama, and subsequently taught at Tougaloo College in Mississippi, found his work challenging and invigorating at these two HBCUs. Monro said in a lecture at Harvard in 1976 that most of the readings used in English classes in Black colleges come from Black authors, and that from time to time he and the class "stop to see how Frederick Douglass or Richard Wright or Martin Luther King, Jr. shaped a given sentence to deal with an idea or a piece of information" (Monro 1978, 242). The rationale for using literature created by Black authors, he said, is for the purpose of helping students and faculty develop a full and accurate awareness of the Black American experience. Since public schools tend not to deal with the Black experience sufficiently, Monro believed it was the colleges' responsibility to "provide basic information about it, telling the truth, and setting the record straight." He also stated that "The country would be much better off if White colleges would do the same," concluding that "the White colleges are not going to do it, or anything like it which is one reason why sensible people prefer to teach in Black schools" (245).

The testimony of John Monro is evidence of the beneficial effect of assembling a diversified faculty at HBCUs. The empathy he developed with his students enhanced them and him. He also became a fulfilled scholar experimenting with different pedagogical approaches to learning that benefited students, the school, and himself.

Since their founding, HBCUs have had multiracial faculties ranging from one-fifth to one-half of their teachers and also multiracial boards of trustees. Charles Merrill, former chair of the Board of Trustees of Morehouse College, said, "A few White southerners taught at the college out of a social or Christian conviction. . . . These were often remarkable individuals" (Merrill 1978, 169). And we say that Charles Merrill, a White philanthropist and educator, was also a remarkable individual.

The commencement address at Morehouse College was delivered by Benjamin Elijah Mays in 1967. He was seventy-two years old and had notified the school that he would retire as president at the end of the school year. Inviting him to deliver the Commencement address was a way of honoring his long and fruitful administration. However, he turned the end of his speech into a celebration of Charles Merrill:

> I can not close this address without publicly paying tribute to Charles Merrill, chairman of the Morehouse Board of Trustees. . . . If the Morehouse salaries are fairly competitive, give large credit to Charles Merrill. If we have sent able students to the best professional and graduate schools, give credit to Charles Merrill through the Early Admissions Program. If our faculty is widely traveled,

salute Charles Merrill. If sixty-odd Morehouse students have studied and traveled in Europe, let us give thanks to Charles Merrill. If Morehouse is on the verge of being accepted as worthy of membership in Phi Beta Kappa, let us take our hats off to Charles Merrill. It had to be an act of God that Charles Merrill came into our lives. (Mays 2002, 172)

As stated earlier, Mays retired in 1967, leaving behind him a college much stronger than the one he found in 1940 when he was appointed president. Merrill resigned from chairmanship of the Board of Trustees of Morehouse College in 1973. He said his policy "was to press for increased student, faculty, and community representation on the Board [and] to make it Blacker and younger." He also said, "It was . . . time for the chairman to be a Black man rather than a White" (Merrill 1978, 172–173, 174). And so, he stepped aside after rendering extraordinary service to the college. This true and inspiring story of a multiracial Board of Trustees and a multiracial faculty at Morehouse College is a model of what higher education can attain when it draws upon resources of all sorts and conditions of people to give direction and support to a teaching and learning enterprise. The evidence presented shows that HBCUs knew the value of diversity in teaching and learning long before the U.S. Supreme Court in *Grutter v. Bollinger* (2003) sanctioned the educational benefits of diversity and the essentiality of it to the educational mission. In this respect, HBCUs were out front waiting for TWIs and other institutions in American society to catch up. How, then, can anyone say that Black colleges and universities are not needed today after pointing the way to the value of diversity for all?

Lenoar Foster, who has studied White faculty members at Black colleges, offers the following findings:

With respect to faculty . . . HBCUs are more racially diverse than predominantly White institutions of higher education. . . . For almost a quarter of a century after the establishment of higher education for African Americans, the majority of administrators and faculty were White. . . . As the Civil Rights Movement of the 1950s, 1960s and 1970s pervaded the national landscape . . . faculty diversity at both private and public Black colleges was enhanced by the presence of young, liberal, and idealistic White faculty who had participated in many of the activities of the movement. . . . [And as Foster, Miller, and Guyden (1999, 190) state,] "faculty diversity facilitates and champions liberation from all sorts of myths and presumed superiorities and inferiorities." (Foster 2001, 626–627)

This is a fitting message to traditionally White institutions to "go and do likewise" with reference to their faculties.

The data presented in this book will indicate that the case for Black colleges and universities can be summarized in a discussion of the benefits of diversity.

It may seem strange that we identify diversity as the mantra of a set of institutions popularly labeled as HBCUs. Nevertheless, it is a fact that HBCUs are more inclusive in the kinds of students who attend them, in the kinds of professors who teach in them, and in the kinds of leaders who have presided over them than any other set of higher education institutions. The concept of diversity as used in this discussion includes but is not limited to race. It is appropriate to call HBCUs inclusive institutions because they enroll students with a wide range of educational and social characteristics and employ a relatively large number of teachers of many different backgrounds to educate students. While we mention Black colleges as carriers of the diversity mantra, we also describe the Black experience in the United States as a manifestation of inclusiveness. These are gifts to the nation from the Black experience.

Diversity provides an inhospitable environment for the development of group stereotypes. Black students know based on the composition of their college communities that ability is not fixed and unchangeable. "They know this because they see on a daily basis students from impoverished backgrounds becoming scholars and leaders on campus. Affluent . . . [Black] students can understand the point of view of poor . . . students, and vice versa, because the person who has experienced socioeconomic opportunities that are different from one's own frequently is a friend—a classmate, possibly a roommate" (Willie 1981a, 7–8).

The argument set forth in this treatise that diversity and inclusiveness are gifts to American society from its community of Black people is parallel to what Benjamin Mays said at a UNCF convocation in New York on March 20, 1955. In his speech entitled "Our Colleges and the Supreme Court Decision," he said that "the charters of many of the . . . [UNCF schools] were all-inclusive from the very start," that "the vast majority of these colleges were interracial in origin." Further, he stated that "the faculties [of these schools] soon became integrated, and . . . have never lost their interracial character" and that these "colleges have carried the torch of freedom and interracial good will." It was his hope back in 1955 that "the Supreme Court decision . . . will enable these colleges in time . . . to . . . open their doors to all qualified students who seek admission" (qtd. in Colston 2002, 45).

It seems to us that now is the time to fulfill the hope that Dr. Mays had for HBCUs a half century ago. Our belief is that education in an inclusive learning environment will benefit White people and Brown people as well as Black people. We know, as stated by Robert Shireman, former director of the higher education program of the James Irving Foundation, that "when presidents and provosts take some responsibility for the . . . vision for change, it makes all the difference in the world." Shireman has urged the leadership of colleges and universities to legitimize the vision of diversity because of his belief that "issues concerning how to sustain and encourage diversity are far from settled on most campuses across America" (Shireman 2002, B10).

HBCUs are urged to revisit and reconfirm their mission for diversity and inclusiveness. Shireman said that "the most common conclusion among colleges [supported by] the Irving Foundation [is] that they need to do more to diversify their faculties" (Shireman 2003, B11). None is better positioned than HBCUs to help all colleges and universities to become diversified and inclusive in their faculty, staff, and board. This is their charge to keep for the society that they inhabit. Some HBCUs are trying hard to maintain and carry forward the themes of diversity and inclusiveness that were first introduced into the nation's system of higher education by these schools. But the number is dwindling, indicating that such schools need help in performing this function.

Huston-Tillotson, Florida Memorial, and Oakland (all HBCUs) are private colleges with significant proportions of students of a race other than Black; student bodies in these schools had proportions that were 24 percent, 17 percent, and 16 percent non-Black, respectively, in 1998. Five other schools—Xavier, St. Augustine's, Paul Quinn, Hampton, and Wiley (also private HBCUs) had student bodies in 1998 in which non-Blacks varied from 10 percent to 14 percent. Only one of these schools, Huston-Tillotson, has surpassed the minimum critical mass level for minority populations of 20 percent; nearly a quarter of its students (24 percent) identified with racial groups other than Black. We know that Florida Memorial and Paul Quinn had special programs that attract Hispanic students. Florida Memorial is located in the northwestern section of Miami, and Paul Quinn is in Dallas, Texas. In addition to its program designed to attract Hispanic students, Florida Memorial also has an aviation center featuring programs in air traffic control, aviation administration, and aviation computer technology. Paul Quinn developed a program designed to attract Hispanics and has a parallel degree program with Texas State Technical Institute. Students from a range of economic backgrounds were attracted to Paul Quinn in 1998 because it had a co-op program that permitted students to work off campus while studying. The same year, Hampton University attracted students from most of the states in the United States. It has four undergraduate schools and one graduate school. The faculty of Hampton has a high level of diversity with a large minority of 45 percent who identify with non-Black racial groups. Moreover, the proportions of men and women on Hampton's faculty are similar to the racial proportions. At Hampton, 13 percent of its students are classified as non-Black. To bring underprepared students up to speed, Hampton has a tutorial program for every department. Hampton has several programs in applied science such as nursing and speech pathology, architecture, and special education. It also has remedial programs in mathematics, reading, and writing. Obviously, an in-depth study is needed to determine how and why some private HBCUs have achieved the student diversity mentioned above and whether the methods used in these schools can be replicated in other private or public HBCUs throughout the nation.

## CONCLUSION

We have focused on diversity in this chapter because HBCUs have always emphasized inclusiveness among faculty members, especially with reference to their racial and ethnic characteristics and to diversity among students in terms of their socioeconomic status, learning styles, and personal preparation for college studies.

Two Supreme Court decisions—*Brown v. Board of Education* in 1954 and *Grutter v. Bollinger* in 2003—have emphasized inclusiveness and diversity in education. In 1954, the unanimous opinion of the Supreme Court announced that segregation in public education "is a denial of the equal protection of the law" and that "'separate but equal' has no place" in public education. In 2003, a majority opinion of the Supreme Court in *Grutter v. Bollinger* mentioned "educational benefits of a diverse student body" and deferred to the plaintiff's judgment that "diversity is essential [to the school's] educational mission."

Since the nation is beginning to value inclusiveness and diversity that HBCUs have advocated since their founding, it is time that these schools show by precept and example how to increase the number of Brown and White students in their student bodies. HBCUs must take leadership in indicating the educational benefits of minority status for non-Black students. As diversity advocates, HBCUs may also benefit themselves by finding new markets from which to recruit students, since a majority of Black students no longer attend predominantly Black schools.

# Chapter Four

# The Case for Black Colleges Today

## THE PURPOSES AND EFFECTS OF HISTORICALLY BLACK COLLEGES AND UNIVERSITIES

In previous chapters, we discussed the educational goals and priorities of Black college presidents and how historically Black colleges and universities (HBCUs)[1] have exemplified the effort to diversify higher education. We now shift our attention to the purposes, benefits, population, and ethical positions of these institutions from their inception to early twenty-first century America.

The question of why Black colleges[2] were founded was tackled at the seminal "Black Colleges as a National Resource: Beyond 1975" conference sponsored by the Southern Educational Foundation in February 1976. The answer was that Black colleges addressed America's refusal to educate young African Americans:[3] "They were established because of the exclusionary practices, systematic patterns of denial, lack of access to existing institutions of higher education, and the multiple realities of insidious, pernicious, and demeaning de jure educational apartheid in the United States. In [then executive director of the United Negro College Fund Christopher] Edley's words, 'they were borne out

---

1 We cite the definition of historically Black colleges and universities (HBCUs) from the National Center for Education Statistics: "institutions established prior to 1964 whose principal mission was, and is, the education of Black Americans" (1994, vii).

2 In this chapter, we use the terms "historically Black colleges" and "Black colleges" interchangeably.

3 In this chapter, we use the definition of term "African American" from the U.S. Census Bureau: "A person having origins in any of the Black racial groups of Africa. It includes people who indicate their race as 'Black, African Am., or Negro,' or provide written entries such as African American, Afro American, Kenyan, Nigerian, or Haitian." We use the term "Black" interchangeably with the words mentioned above.

of necessity; they arose as a humanitarian response to the educational needs of black people.' They were founded, as [Kenneth] Tollett asserted, 'at a time when no one else would serve this (educational) need'" (Blackwell 1976, 9).

Blackwell reported in 1976 that 80 percent of college graduates of African descent were educated at Black colleges and that these institutions "helped to establish certain practical areas of knowledge as legitimate spheres of academic and scientific inquiry within the broader educational community," such as the race relations institutes founded at Fisk University and Virginia Union University (Blackwell 1976, 13).

Today, though 80 percent of African-American collegians are enrolled in predominantly White institutions, HBCUs account for one-fourth of the nation's African-American graduates (Hrabowski 2002; Brown and Freeman 2002). The innovations at Black colleges have also garnered recognition at the highest political levels. In 1993, President Bill Clinton launched a White House Initiative on Historically Black Colleges and Universities, stating that "Historically black colleges and universities continue to play a vital role by adding to the diversity and caliber of the Nation's higher education system. Furthermore, these institutions remind all Americans of our obligations to uphold the principles of justice and equality enshrined in our Constitution" (U.S. Department of Education 1997, 1).

President George W. Bush signed a new executive order and pledged to increase funding for HBCUs and Historically Black Graduate Institutions (HBGIs) by 30 percent between 2001 and 2005 (U.S. Department of Education 2002b). While a 5 percent increase for historically Black and Hispanic-serving colleges was proposed in the 2004 budget, there has been criticism for the administration's failure to deal with recommendations issued in September 2002 by a blue-ribbon panel on Black colleges (Wickham 2003).

## CHANGES TO THE VALIDITY OF PURPOSES AT HISTORICALLY BLACK COLLEGES AND UNIVERSITIES

From the record of HBCUs and the statements of two U.S. presidents, one might expect that the future of historically Black colleges and universities would be fixed in the American pantheon of higher educational institutions. However, arguments that are similar to those made in the 1970s continue to be voiced in opposition to the existence of Black colleges. The U.S. Supreme Court took a divergent view from the executive branch in *U.S. v. Fordice.* In 1992, the Supreme Court held that HBCUs are a vestige of segregation and that the State of Mississippi must either eliminate them or find a compelling educational justification for their existence (Wenglinsky 1997).

This reasoning is flawed. First, there are many institutions in American society that exist as a vestige of segregation. For instance, women's colleges were founded because at that time women were not welcome in men's colleges. Some of these women's colleges continue to exist. To single out Black colleges for eradication because of the nature of their origin seems unjust. A quarter of a century ago, Benjamin Mays observed that "No one has ever said that Catholic colleges should be abolished because they are Catholic. Nobody says that Brandeis and Albert Einstein must die because they are Jewish. Nobody says that Lutheran and Episcopalian schools should not be because they are Lutheran and Episcopalian. Why should Howard University be abolished because it is known as a black university? Why pick out Negro colleges and say they must die? Blot out these colleges; you blot out the image of black men and women in education" (Mays 1978, 26–27).

The court failed to realize that actions such as Governor Ross Barnett standing in the doorway of Ole Miss in 1962 were the true vestige of segregation. No one stood in the doorway of HBCUs such as Jackson State or Mississippi Valley State to prevent desegregation. In fact, research points to compelling educational justifications for HBCUs:

[There is] a benefit provided by Historically Black Colleges and Universities not provided by Traditionally White Institutions—they prepare Black students for careers in the sciences and engineering, professions in which they are most underrepresented. . . . Because students often cite cost as a reason for choosing Historically Black Colleges and Universities and because so many come from families of low socio-economic status, it is probable that many students would not have attended any college at all had there not been a Historically Black College to attend. The benefits of Historically Black Colleges and Universities, then, accrue not only to students who choose them over Traditionally White Institutions, but also to students who choose them over moving directly into the job market. (Wenglinsky 1997)

Such justifications help to explain why the senior author of this book declared Black colleges and universities "the research and development arm of higher education," noting that the institutions "have experimented with ways of effectively involving students in governance and in relevant community services. They were among the first to implement open-admissions policies. They demonstrated that classical and career educations can be united within a single curriculum. They established . . . faculty [mentors] for promising students. These and other innovations now have been adopted by other colleges and universities" (Willie 1981a, 105).

The attention HBCUs give to individual students is perhaps best illustrated in the case of Mike Foster, who was a student at the Southern University Law

Center in Louisiana. The state's other law school at Louisiana State University sity requires that first-year students refrain from working, which made Foster ineligible to enroll there. However, Southern Law Center offers a part-time program that suited Foster, who continued to work while pursuing his degree. What makes Foster's situation so interesting is that aside from being a White male, at the time of his enrollment he was seventy years old and the incumbent governor of Louisiana. He praised the Southern Law Center for offering him the opportunity to study, stating that "I'm very comfortable going there. I wear my blue jeans to class, and everyone really goes out of their way to make me feel like I fit in" (qtd. in Dyer 2003, 8). Surely, an institution that provides opportunity for individuals of differing socioeconomic classes, races, occupations, and age groups is sorely needed in higher education today.

As Kannerstein notes, "the concern of black colleges is not who gets in but what happens to them afterward" (Kannerstein 1978, 37). These institutions wish to serve students as well as their communities and to "liberate [them] while teaching a lesson to the rest of the academic community" about inclusion (50).

## CURRICULUM AND PEDAGOGY

The nation's 105 HBCUs offer a myriad of curricula. From liberal arts institutions such as Pennsylvania's Lincoln University to highly technical campuses such as Alabama's Tuskegee University, the types of courses offered allow students instruction in virtually any field of endeavor.

### Curricular History

At first glance, the debate between Black educators William Edward Burghardt Du Bois and Booker Taliafero Washington in the early twentieth century seemed to be a presentation of "warring ideologies" (Hedgepeth, Edmonds, and Craig 1978, 17). However, a closer examination of the Washington-Du Bois debate, as mentioned in chapter 2, indicates some commonality between the two educators' positions. While Washington's belief is commonly presented as stating that Blacks should gravitate toward industrial education (Anderson 1988) and Du Bois's belief is presented as embracing a liberal education focused on advancing the cause of franchisement and civil rights (Du Bois 1903), Hedgepeth, Edmonds, and Craig (1978, 17) note that "These 'warring ideologies . . .' have subsequently come together so at present black colleges intertwine social, vocational and academic programs in their overall mission to educate for 'leadership in democracy.'"

It appears that the direct effect of the Washington-Du Bois debate influenced historically Black colleges to integrate liberal arts and industrial education. The effects of these "warring ideologies" are evident in McBay's (1978) essay "Black Students in the Sciences: A Look at Spelman College." McBay describes Spelman as a liberal arts college for women that created a division of natural sciences in 1972. Twenty-seven years later, Dr. Mae Jamison, the first Black woman astronaut and a Spelman alumna, traveled into space. By 1995, Spelman was one of six institutions designated by the National Science Foundation (NSF) and the National Aeronautics and Space Administration (NASA) as a Model Institution for Excellence in undergraduate science and math education (Spelman College 2003). Spelman, like many Black colleges, has chosen to educate students in both the humanities and the sciences and has excelled at this task.

## A Higher Curricular Calling

Another important factor to consider when analyzing the curriculum at historically Black colleges is the mission of these institutions. Black Americans were, and currently are, in many ways dependent on historically Black colleges to produce men and women to serve as the vanguard of the community. This sentiment is perhaps best expressed in the words of a 1945 speech by Dr. Benjamin E. Mays, the sixth president of Morehouse College: "It will not be sufficient for Morehouse College . . . to produce clever graduates, men fluent in speech and able to argue their way through; but rather honest men, men who are sensitive to the wrongs, the sufferings and the injustices of society and who are willing to accept responsibility for correcting the ills" (qtd. in Willie 1979, 47).

Mays called on both the students and faculty of Morehouse to steadfastly focus beyond facts and figures and to dedicate themselves to lives of community and public service. Perhaps the best example of this can be found in the life of his protégé, Dr. Martin Luther King Jr., who referred to himself as a "drum major for justice, peace, and righteousness" (King 1968a). In an essay entitled "The Black College in Higher Education" written shortly before his passing, Mays restated that Black colleges gave students an additional curricular focus on the accomplishments and needs of Black Americans:

> The black colleges have a double role. They must be as much concerned with Shakespeare, Tennyson, and Marlowe as the white colleges. But the Negro institutions must give equal emphasis to the writing of Paul Dunbar, Countee Cullen, and Langston Hughes; as much emphasis as white colleges to white sociologists, but equal attention to black sociologists like E. Franklin Frazier and Charles S. Johnson. The black colleges must include works of great white historians like Schlesinger and Toynbee, but they must also include the works of John Hope

Franklin, Carter G. Woodson, and Charles Wesley. It is not enough for black colleges to teach their students the economics of capitalism. The graduate of a black college must also understand the problems of the small black capitalist and be able to help him and must know something about cooperatives. These examples are what I mean by the double role of Negro colleges. (Mays 1978, 28)

Dr. Mays clearly made the connection between the role of Black colleges in supporting the "double consciousness" of African Americans that W. E. B. Du Bois conceptualized in the early twentieth century. Similarly, Dr. Samuel DuBois Cook, the sixth president of Dillard University, reiterated the higher curricular calling of historically Black colleges in an essay titled "The Socio-Ethical Role and Responsibility of Black College Graduates," stating that "the black college has the same general mission as a white college, but, additionally, the black college has a special and unique purpose. The black college, thus, has a dual mission. It is about human excellence, the superior education and training of tender minds, nourishment of the creative imagination, and reverence for learning; it is also about the development of moral character and the production of better men and women for a more humane, decent, and open world" (Cook 1978, 55).

Historically Black college leaders, then, embody and articulate Hedgepeth, Edmonds, and Craig's schema of "not [providing] education for its own sake but for a continual challenge of the status quo in oppressive race relations and social behavior" (Hedgepeth, Edmonds, and Craig 1978, 18). It is not a surprise, then, that many of this nation's preeminent leaders who worked toward improving race relations and social behavior, such as Jesse Jackson, Barbara Jordan, Rosa Parks, Marian Wright Edelman, Martin Luther King Jr., Andrew Young, Ruth Simmons, and John Hope Franklin, are graduates of historically Black colleges. These men and women learned the lessons of high moral character to improve their communities, the nation, and the world.

Given the praise afforded by these scholars concerning the curricular approaches at historically Black colleges and universities, we should next turn our attention to the pedagogical techniques at these institutions. How are relations constructed between faculty and students, and what teaching methods are embraced by Black colleges?

## THE PROFESSORATE

An often-overlooked strength of HBCUs is the faculty at these institutions. Despite a historic lack of equitable resources and facilities, educators in Black schools are primarily responsible for the emergence of an educated, professional middle class (Cecelski 1994; Anderson 1988). Black teachers have held esteemed positions in their communities, due to the importance that Blacks have placed on education (Cecelski 1994; Willie and Reddick 2003). This is especially true in higher education. As Daniel Thompson (1978) notes, HBCUs have managed to produce, attract, and retain a core of great teachers over the years.

Thompson's (1978) descriptive statistics of the Black college professorate illustrates a diverse population among race and gender. He reported that 40 percent of Black college teachers were female, and between 25 and 50 percent of the faculty were White. Thompson also found that HBCU faculties tended to emphasize classroom activities, personal counseling, and sponsoring student organizations. His analysis further established that most top faculty members at HBCUs taught entry-level classes, because these faculty members want to ensure that students receive the best foundational instruction so that their subsequent academic experiences will be effective.

Almost twenty years later, Cose (1997) reported a similar philosophy toward teaching at Xavier University. Under the leadership of Dr. Norman Francis, Xavier was the top-ranked university in the number of baccalaureate degrees granted to African-American students in biological and life sciences, as well as in the physical sciences, in the academic year 1999–2000. Equally impressive is the fact that from 1996 to 2001, Xavier sent more African-American students to medical school than any other institution (Stewart 2001). Such impressive outcomes, however, are only possible when faculty is dedicated to working closely with students.

This approach has been highly effective and, as this vignette from a Xavier graduate illustrates, perhaps rivals some of the teaching techniques at some of the nations' top schools: "During his first year at Harvard Medical School, Keith Amos was more than popular—he was needed. Amos quickly became the histology gem of his class. While his classmates struggled, Amos cruised through the microscopic study of tissue structure. 'I had been taught histology so well in undergraduate school that, frankly, I already knew the material,' says Amos. So he ended up tutoring his classmates. 'They asked me for help, and I was happy to do it,' said Amos. 'I enjoyed telling my Harvard classmates that I had attended a small Black university'" (Stewart 2001, 22).

This intentional pedagogical approach that takes the most talented faculty members and links them to incoming students differs from the model observed at many predominantly White institutions, where entry-level courses are often taught by graduate students and junior faculty. Black colleges understand that this model often does not serve students well and have chosen to buck the trend established by other colleges.

Lest one believe that innovative pedagogical practices exist only in the sciences, Charles U. Smith (1978) detailed advances in the social sciences. In an essay titled "Teaching and Learning Social Sciences in Black Universities," Smith lays out activities designed to help students and faculty in the combined goals of furthering knowledge and research in the field and serving the community at Florida Agricultural and Mechanical University (FAMU). A field experience program gives students internship opportunities that brings them into contact with real issues of human welfare. In addition, a service center in a nearby community helps to connect community activists and students. While Smith is clear in stating that the faculty at FAMU does not function under the "publish or perish" dictum, he states that professors feel that membership on boards and journals helps to motivate students to achieve the same goal.

## ETHICS IN THE HBCU CURRICULUM

HBCUs have examined ethical dimensions that many types of institutions perhaps have not. As Charles Verharen observed, "*Veritas* may very well serve Harvard University as a motto, but HBCU's must go far beyond that to *veritas et utilitas* (the motto of Howard University)." In other words, HBCU graduates are charged with a responsibility to address problems and dilemmas that other institutions are unlikely to. In this vision, utility is parallel to truth. Verharen further illuminates this point by stating that HBCUs "have a moral responsibility to furnish curricula that focus students' attention on problems that may escape the concentration of other institutions" (Verharen 1993, 200).

This vision is well demonstrated by the example of Clark Atlanta University, which was recognized in the mid-1990s for garnering more than $35 million in federal science and engineering grants (Burd 1995). Commenting on the success of Clark Atlanta, vice president for research and sponsored programs Kofi Bota, states that "I truly believe that if provided appropriate support on the national level, a few historically Black colleges—Clark Atlanta, Howard University, Florida A&M and North Carolina A&T—could develop into nationally ranked universities, and at the same time address the needs of the African-American community" (qtd. in Burd 1995). Bota's words clearly delineate that it is not enough for HBCUs to simply become nationally ranked institutions; they must also reach an ethical goal of serving the needs of Black Americans. Specifically, Clark Atlanta initiated a number of projects to study how environmental pollution affects African-American communities. These projects also focused on solutions to the problem.

The commitment to infusing the curriculum with *utilitas* is also evident when one peruses the degree requirements for students enrolled in the Department of Business Administration at Morehouse College. One of the required courses, Legal Environment of Business, is described as "focus[ing] on the government's regulation of business through public law and provides an overview of *social responsibility, ethics,* policy and economics as they relate to the regulation of business" (DEBA 2003, emphasis added). For Morehouse, it is vital that business students are exposed to issues of ethics in business before earning a degree.

The recent *New York Times* scandal involving Jayson Blair, a rising reporter who was discovered fabricating news articles, has prompted a discussion on teaching ethics at historically Black colleges. At Florida A&M University where faculty were considering a proposal to eliminate the journalistic ethics course, the Journalism Department chair James Hawkins advocated keeping the current ethics course intact: "There are many issues of an ethical nature that journalism students should be aware of—privacy, conflicts of interest, use of anonymous sources, misrepresentation, misinformation—all of these are ethical issues" (qtd. in Walker 2003). Hawkins's interest in keeping the ethical emphasis in curriculum is one shared by many journalism professors at other Black institutions. It is fortunate that Black colleges are discussing how professional behavior may be enhanced by courses on ethics in the curriculum.


## BEING OPEN TO ALL STILL MEANS EXCELLENCE

Some Black colleges are open enrollment institutions, and still others admit students who would not be considered competitive at other institutions due to their low standardized test scores. This is a fact well known to those who study higher education. HBCUs acknowledge the contributing factors in students' lives that may lead to seemingly poor academic performance. They also have faith in their students' potential and attempt to strengthen their potential in summer prep programs. "Most of these students [at Xavier's summer prep program for high school students] may not be candidates for the Ivy League, but if they show some potential (especially if they are male, since a substantial majority of participants are female), Xavier tends to take them. 'Is it fair to eliminate someone or not give a kid a chance just because [he or she] went to a lousy high school? Or just because [some students] were poor? Or because [they had] a lousy adviser?' [premed adviser Dr. J. W.] Carmichael asked" (Cose 1997, 59).

In this vignette, Carmichael illustrates the importance of student potential over high school performance, socioeconomic status, or the quality of advising received before college. The problem of minority student underperformance still exists in the nation's K–12 schools (Bowen and Bok 1998), and many HBCUs evaluate students with this fact in mind and are willing to give such students a chance.

This is not to say that all students enrolled and admitted to HBCUs are not stellar students before, during, and after their college years. The example of Xavier University's premed programs placing more Black students in medical school than any other institution of higher education has previously been cited in this book (Stewart 2001). In 2001, Florida A&M University was the second greatest recruiter of Black National Achievement Scholars, recruiting three fewer scholars than the number one university, Harvard, and besting Stanford, Yale, and the University of Florida. FAMU was number one in recruitment of such scholars in 1992, 1995, 1997, and 2000 (Black Excel 2002).

In considering the power and intentionality of the curriculum and pedagogical practices of HBCUs, it is appropriate to return to the words of Dr. Benjamin E. Mays: "I had learned through my own experience that I could compete successfully in a white man's world. Thus the role of the black colleges and their continuing existence has never been a problem to me. I have never been deceived into believing that black colleges are interim institutions that would go out of existence when white colleges became liberal enough to accept Negroes without discriminating against them. I have argued for as long as I can remember that the image of the black man and woman in education and their contribution to American life must be equated with the black colleges" (Mays 1978, 22).

## FACULTY AT HISTORICALLY BLACK COLLEGES AND UNIVERSITIES

As we review the literature on Black colleges, a recurring area of interest is the faculty that teaches at these institutions. Again, history and necessity have shaped the teaching faculties at HBCUs in radically different ways in comparison to predominantly White institutions. Though there are several differences of note, one predominant finding is the tendency of HBCUs to make claims to their excellence through the strength and skill of faculty as pedagogues, while predominantly White institutions may tend to rest their reputations on the test scores and class ranking of their students (Flacks and Thomas 1998).

## FACULTY COMPOSITION AT BLACK COLLEGES: AN OVERVIEW

As Thompson notes, Black colleges, public and private, have historically received "only the crumbs from the tables of this nation's educational funds" (Thompson 1978, 183). Therefore, teachers and professors at such institutions must be motivated for reasons beyond financial gain, evidenced by the words of Benjamin E. Mays: "It wasn't affluence . . . it was a few able, dedicated teachers . . . who widened the Negro's horizon and made him believe that he could do big and worthwhile things. . . . Salaries were miserably low, but devotion was correspondingly high" (qtd. in Thompson 1978, 178).

While early studies reported a gap between the educational attainment of Black college faculty and faculty at predominantly White colleges, Bowles and DeCosta reported in 1971 that "many of the observed differences between historically Negro colleges and historically White colleges are more a function of size and financial support than they are a function of race" (qtd. in Newby 1982, 12).

Newby's analysis of research on Black college faculty recognizes that the earliest efforts started in the first decade of the twentieth century, leading to a landmark comparative analysis of Black institutions and predominantly White colleges by Earl Huyck in 1966. Huyck's data showed that 53 percent of Black college faculty were teaching first- and second-year students, compared to 41 percent in White colleges. Five percent of Black college faculty were primarily teaching graduate students, compared to 19 percent of White college faculty. Huyck's study revealed interesting findings about the composition of Black college faculties; in 1962–1963, Black colleges had twice the proportion of women faculty members and had more older faculty members when compared to predominantly White colleges (Newby 1982). A more recent study reported that women composed 40 percent of the professorate in Black colleges (Roebuck and Murty 1993).

A study conducted by Smith and Borgstedt of White faculty member at six HBCUs found that 19–40 percent of faculty at those institutions were White. Smith and Borgstedt note the unique position of Black colleges in American higher education: "The Black college campus is an interesting laboratory for the study of interracial interaction. White faculty who have been socialized in a majority role are abruptly assuming a minority role within the Black institution" (Smith and Borgstedt 1985, 149). This statement speaks volumes about the experiences of White faculty at Black colleges. As the senior author of this book notes, the experience of living within two cultures can result in enhanced opportunity for all: "Based on my analysis of the great liberation leaders in the world throughout history, I have found many of them are immersed in two different cultures. . . . So now I asked, 'How are Whites ever going to be liberation leaders for their people unless they have the same experiences of immersion in different cultures?' That is what is behind my call for Black colleges to embrace both Blacks and Whites so that [Whites] can learn the way of life of another culture" (qtd. in Matthews 1999, 25).

Even among faculty identifying themselves as White, there was further diversity. At some campuses, up to 30 percent of the White faculty members were internationally born, leading Smith and Borgstedt to comment that "Whites are obviously better represented in Black colleges than Blacks are in White colleges" (Smith and Borgstedt 1985, 154–155). This trend remains true to the present day (Cole 1993).

In 1995 the nation's 26,835 Black faculty constituted roughly 58 percent of all full-time faculty at four-year HBCUs (Fields 2000), meaning that non-Black faculty comprised 42 percent of the full-time faculty at those institutions. In comparison, African-American, Hispanic, Asian, and American Indian/Alaskan Native faculty members account for a total of 13.4 percent of full-time faculty, and White faculty account for 83.9 percent of full-time faculty at all other postsecondary institutions, according to 1997 data from the U.S. Department of Education (Anon. 2000a). Numerous studies, then, establish the fact that Black colleges present faculty diversity to a significant degree (Roebuck and Murty 1993), a finding echoed in Outcalt and Skewes-Cox's (2002) study of student engagement at HBCUs. They found that 65 percent of HBCU students reported that they were "satisfied" or "very satisfied" with the ethnic/racial diversity of their faculty, compared with only 24 percent of African-American students at traditionally White institutions (TWIs).

## The Work of Faculty at Historically Black Colleges

Thompson details the work of faculty at Black colleges in the essay "Black College Faculty and Students: The Nature of Their Interaction." Noting that HBCUs have always worked to transform socioeconomically and academically struggling students into leaders in the professions, business, and public affairs, Thompson states, "Since Black colleges have never had the funds and influence to adequately support this urgent mission an uncommonly heavy burden has fallen upon the faculty" (Thompson 1978, 188). The range of needs of Black students requires a faculty that excels in the art of teaching above all else. At their beginning and to this day, Black colleges have emphasized creative teaching, described in chapter 2 and the following example.

The aforementioned John Monro, a former dean of Harvard College who devoted many years to teaching at Miles College in Alabama and Tougaloo College in Mississippi, detailed the origin of this pedagogical philosophy. He was impressed with Jean Piaget's philosophy of moving from concrete knowledge to abstract concepts. These ideas figure heavily in the teaching methods of Monro. "Our task is to work with [students] where they are, by reference to details, to specifics, by giving them practice in induction in discovery, in drawing their own conclusions. Certainly we will do them no good by lecturing to them in traditional, professional generalities" (Monro 1978, 244). Monro further cites Floyd Nordland's application of Piaget's theories as a major influence on the teaching staff at Miles. The works of Arthur Whimbey, a psychologist who wrote *Intelligence Can Be Taught,* also has had a significant impact on pedagogy at Miles College in Alabama as well as at Xavier University in Louisiana.

Cose (1997) details the rise of Xavier's science education program that has sent many Black students to medical school (Stewart 2001). Thirty years ago, Xavier's science program was "solidly second rate" (Cose 1997, 53). Xavier's president, Norman C. Francis, appointed J. W. Carmichael, a chemistry professor, to serve as the university's premed advisor and charged Carmichael with the task of raising achievement in the sciences at Xavier. Like Monro, Carmichael discovered the work of Whimbey, which focuses on a group-centered, problem-solving approach to difficult problems. Carmichael and the Xavier faculty worked with Whimbey to develop a teaching philosophy that is based on rigor, remediation, and reasoning.

The results of the Whimbey-influenced teaching methods adopted by the faculties of Miles and Xavier have been impressive. Monro used similar methods at Tougaloo College and reported that this partially open enrollment school placed 10 percent of its graduates in medical schools (Shores 1979). Xavier's success is legend: beyond the previously reported fact that it sent more African-American students to medical school than any other institution in the latter half of the 1990s, 93 percent of its students who enter medical school graduate (Stewart 2001).

A number of factors are at work at these institutions to provide such results. Above all, a dedicated faculty devoted to the enterprise of teaching students is essential. As Monro notes, such programs "need . . . teachers who care enough about students to see them as individuals and work with them as individuals (Monro 1978, 248).

Much of the motivation for the work of faculty members at HBCUs comes from a sense of greater purpose. Roebuck and Murty's survey of faculty at HBCUs found that Black professors at those institutions saw themselves as mentors, role models, and surrogate parents for Black youth. They provide assistance and support, and they serve as educational liaisons between the campus and community and as agents of change in a racially segregated society. Similarly, Johnetta Cole, Spelman College president emeritus, sees teachers as mentors and role models: "The women and men of the Spelman faculty are seriously committed to the education of these young women. . . . At Spelman, students see individuals who look like them serving as the president of the college, a professor of biology or economics" (qtd. in Cole 1993, 180).

## Faculty Mentoring at Black Colleges

Perhaps the sense of greater purpose is best illustrated by examples of professors who served as mentors to students. Willie details such an example in the life story of the historian John Hope Franklin. Originally planning to be a lawyer, Franklin's future plans were significantly altered when he studied under Theodore Currier, a young White professor at Fisk University. Franklin recalled that Currier "discovered that I had some promise, and he nurtured me to attend Harvard. . . . I had never had such an intellectual experience." Franklin indeed applied to Harvard and was accepted for graduate study, but the economic hardships of the Depression made it impossible for Franklin's family to support him. When this news reached Currier, he declared, "Money will not keep you from going to Harvard!" Currier invited Franklin back to Nashville, where the two men sought funding from many sources. When this effort failed, Currier, who had completed his third year teaching at Fisk at age thirty-three, went to the bank and borrowed enough money to pay for Franklin's first year at Harvard. Franklin was not the only student Currier assisted. The historian L. D. Reddick and the lawyer Wade McCree also benefited from Currier's munificence. The example of Theodore Currier exemplifies the best of mentoring, as Franklin reminisced: "Currier was my closest friend. We started out in a student-teacher relationship but became very close friends" (qtd. in Willie 1986, 18–19).

Another example of the power of mentoring that Black college faculty and administrators provide for their students can be found in Benjamin Mays's 1971 autobiography *Born to Rebel*. Mays recounts an excerpt from Dr. Martin Luther King Jr.'s *Stride Toward Freedom* in which King describes a meeting held by his father, the Reverend Martin Luther King Sr., and several community elders in Atlanta. Concerned about the younger King's safety after several leaders of the Montgomery bus boycott had been arrested, the elder Reverend King and his peers appealed to his son to stay away from Montgomery for a time. Overcome with emotion, King Jr. replied that he had to return to Montgomery even if he were put in jail, to suffer with the people who had invested so much faith in his leadership: "In the moment of silence that followed, I heard my father break into tears. I looked at Doctor Mays, one of the great influences in my life. Perhaps he heard my unspoken plea. At any rate, he was soon defending my position strongly." Mays states, "I had to defend Martin Luther's position. Here was a man of deep integrity and firm convictions" (Mays 1971, 268). Tellingly, it was his mentor who recognized the importance of making that statement and supporting the young Martin Luther King's decision to lead at a time when he was most needed.

In a survey study, Willie, Grady, and Hope (1991) discussed the assets and liabilities of graduate study at HBCUs. They found that Black graduate students were satisfied with their opportunities to serve as teaching assistants at predominantly Black graduate schools. However, the students stated that they had inadequate opportunities to collaborate with faculty on research projects. This is perhaps explained by Thompson's study, which suggests that faculty at Black colleges juggle classroom activities, personal counseling, and sponsoring student organizations, leaving little, if any, time for research or writing. While the demands on the time of Black college faculty are serious problems for graduate students, Thompson tell us that "The work of talented, dedicated, persevering teachers has substantiated the claim of Black colleges that they can take certain students who are rejected by most or all of the affluent, high-ranking, prestigious white colleges and produce a relatively larger proportion of top-flight college graduates" (Thompson 1978, 192).

After reviewing the gathering of elders to advise Martin Luther King Jr., we also may conclude that faculty and administrators in Black colleges help their protégés to become good and responsible citizens as well as good scholars.

## EMPHASIZING THE STRENGTH OF SCHOLARS OVER STUDENTS

Mentoring and modeling roles are mentioned often in this chapter, because most Black colleges believe that a school is no better than its teachers. This assertion represents a fundamental difference Blacks and Whites have in their assessments of the ingredients of a good school. Whites tend to characterize a school as excellent because of the kinds of students it attracts, while Blacks tend to characterize a school as excellent because of the kinds of teachers it has. This fundamental difference between Black and White educational institutions is seldom acknowledged. Many institutions still boast about the average SAT and ACT scores for their entering class, although numerous studies prove that these measures offer only a slight correlation to students' first-semester performance and little else (Baron and Norman 1992; Vars and Bowen 1998; Perez 2002). Perhaps these institutions would be better served by informing applicants and their families of the level of care and concern by faculty for each student admitted. This is the philosophy of education of most HBCUs, which is different from the philosophy of education of many TWIs.

## ATTITUDES AND ASPIRATIONS OF STUDENTS AT HBCUS

Perhaps the most significant contribution of Black colleges is the development of the students that these institutions serve. Today, nearly three hundred thousand students attend historically Black colleges (Tom Joyner Foundation and William J. Clinton Presidential Foundation 2001). Despite challenges to HBCU enrollment posed by increased competition from predominantly White institutions and the dwindling availability of financial aid dollars to low-income students, Black colleges are reporting enrollments today that are very close to those predicted by the Carnegie Commission in 1971 (Carter-Williams 1984, 223).

The Higher Education Research Institute at the University of California, Los Angeles, disaggregated responses among participating historically Black colleges from the 1996 Annual Freshman Survey (Drewry and Doermann 2001). These findings reveal that students at these institutions are more similar than not, compared to their counterparts at predominantly White institutions. In categories such as age, political stance, and future goals, students at HBCUs responded similarly to their peers at predominantly White schools. However, among students at private Black colleges, a greater percentage stated that they intended to pursue an advanced degree, to be authorities in their field of choice, to be successful in their own businesses, to be community leaders, and to help others in difficulty. Another interesting finding is that in 1995, in comparison to all freshmen at private four-year colleges, more Black students at HBCUs expressed a goal of planning to earn a PhD or EdD degree: 27 percent at private Black colleges and 22 percent at public Black colleges, compared to 17 percent at all private four-year colleges. These differences in educational goals, entrepreneurship, and community service suggest that the "value added" at Black colleges is the encouragement and development of such attitudes as mentioned above. These attitudes and aspirations could benefit White students who enroll in HBCUs.

## MARGINALITY AND BICULTURALITY

One novel approach in the effort to highlight the accomplishments and necessity of Black colleges is expanding the benefits of these institutions to non-African-American students. Much has been written in this book detailing the excellent teaching and mentoring that takes place at HBCUs and indicating that any student enrolled in one of these institutions would have the same access to faculty and support that Black students have had over the years. As Black colleges, unlike many predominantly White institutions, have never prohibited student enrollment due to race or national origin, this is a well-practiced actuality (Smiles 2001). The changing characteristics of students attending Black colleges are most evident in those institutions that have become 30 percent or more White in recent years (Levinson 2000). Examples of these schools are Bluefield State College (West Virginia), Bowie State College (Maryland), Kentucky State

University, Delaware State University, and Lincoln University (Missouri). The White students attending such institutions are older (age twenty years and over), more independent, and career oriented. The majority of them work full-time and are enrolled in graduate programs. They tend to commute, are married, and do not rely on their parents for financial support (Carter-Williams 1984, 229).

The unique qualities of Black colleges have made them more attractive to White students, evidenced by the increase in enrollment for this population. In 1976, 9.5 percent of students at historically Black colleges were White. By 1994, the percentage had increased to 13 percent (36,000), according to a study conducted by the National Center for Educational Statistics (1988). By the year 2000, the non-Black component of four-year degree-granting colleges and universities (including White and Brown students) was 14.2 percent (U.S. Department of Education 2002a, 269). This diversity policy has benefited many people beyond the Black American community: "Native American, African, Asian, Latin American, and Caribbean students have all benefited from the educational and social commitment of HBCUs, as well as White women and Jews who enrolled in professional schools at these institutions when gender-, religion- and race-based quotas kept many of them out of traditionally White institutions (TWIs) in significant numbers. . . . During [World War II], refugee scholars from Europe joined the faculties of Atlanta, Fisk, Howard, Xavier, Lincoln, and other schools after arriving in the United States" (Allen and Jewell 2002, 255).

It is no surprise, then, that scholars have encouraged Black colleges to seek out a diverse student body and deliberately invite non-Black students to enroll. Indeed, Black colleges and diverse student populations often provide mutual benefits for one another. Lee Monroe, president of Paul Quinn College, initiated a campaign to recruit Hispanic students to this HBCU in Dallas, Texas, by offering scholarships, hiring Mexican American faculty and staff, and encouraging the campus community to learn Spanish and observe Mexican-American holidays (Pego 1995). Citing a need to prepare students for the diverse workplace and to attract students, many of whom are similarly first-generation collegians, Monroe eloquently explains why he has invested Paul Quinn in this effort: "It's just something I believe in. Every person who is well educated must learn to deal with many differences and similarities in the people who are around us. Institutions must reach out and pull in the people who are around them. One of the tremendous services that we can offer because of our historical Black college nature is to bring people together to reduce tensions. Then, nobody feels displaced by the other" (qtd. in Pego 1995, 9).

It is that nature of the historically Black college that the senior author harkens to when he observes that the work of Black colleges is unknown to the general public due to the fact that their image is based on stereotypes and arcane images, and that Whites would better know and promote the cause of these institutions if they experienced attending a Black college: "Whites are more inclined to believe what it is like to be Black in America and what it is like to be educated in Black schools if the report is made by a member of their own race" (Willie 1994a, 155).

Similarly, Allen and Jewell observe that HBCUs have been at the forefront of managing difference among higher education institutions but "are . . . called upon to provide leadership and to make important contributions in the quest for a truly inclusive society. The more complicated landscape of 'difference' in contemporary society challenges HBCUs to do a better job of valuing and incorporating women, gays, lesbians, Asians, Latinos, Muslims, Jews, Whites, and the less affluent" (Allen and Jewell 2002, 255).

Some scholars express concern with the philosophy that Willie, Allen, and Jewell express. They point to trends such as those reported by the National Association for Equal Opportunity in Higher Education (NAFEO) in 2000, when the organization reported that Blacks were in the minority at four HBCUs (the aforementioned Bluefield State College in West Virginia, West Virginia State College, Lincoln University in Missouri, and Shelton State Community College in Alabama) and that a dozen other schools reported White populations from 16 to 49 percent (Anon. 2000b). Paul Delaney, a journalist and chair emeritus of the University of Alabama's journalism department, remarks that action is needed to preserve Black colleges: "If we fail to take action, the twenty-first century will present us with more Bluefield States. And if more Bluefield States means fewer Black college graduates, that will be to the shame of us all" (qtd. in Delaney 1998).

It should be noted, however, that examples such as Bluefield State are the exception. Furthermore, as former United Negro College Fund (UNCF) president William H. Gray III notes, it is the ability of these institutions to meet the needs of students that has resulted in their popularity among people outside the African American community (Anon. 2000b). During a time when many Black colleges are struggling to maintain enrollments, it seems more important than ever to extend the opportunity for a modestly priced, quality education to as many students as are interested. Black colleges have a proud legacy that will not diminish with the addition of students who do not identify as being African American.

## CASE STUDIES OF WHITE STUDENTS AT BLACK COLLEGES

Some previous studies have looked at the experiences of White students at Black colleges. Nixon and Henry (1992) surveyed White students at nine historically Black campuses and found that students were rarely the victims of racial prejudice and reported generally positive experiences at their campuses. Hazzard's (1988) study of White students at two Black colleges revealed that most of these students attended the college solely to get an education, a majority transferred from predominantly White institutions, and over half were satisfied with their educational experience at the Black college. Recent news media, however, provides us with two vignettes of White students at Black colleges.

The example of former Louisiana governor Mike Foster has been previously introduced in this paper. Foster's enrollment created significant media attention and highlighted Southern's law school (Dyer 2001). Foster reported that his experience at Southern had been a positive one: "I am still very appreciative that they gave me an opportunity. The funny thing is that's what Southern is all about, giving opportunities to people who otherwise wouldn't have had them. They gave me an opportunity that nobody else would, and I appreciate it" (qtd. in Dyer 2001, 26). By all accounts, the former governor was held to the same attendance and performance standards as all other students.

Political opponents attempted to create a controversy over Foster's matriculation as a Southern University Law Center student. For instance, Foster was admitted despite a less than stellar LSAT performance. B. K. Agnihotri, the school's chancellor, explained that no minimum LSAT score was required of any applicant to Southern University Law Center and that, in the past, requirements have been waived for exceptional students. For instance, an unnamed civil rights leader was admitted under similar circumstances (Dyer 2001).

The example of Governor Mike Foster underscores the argument Willie and others have made in support of admitting non-Black students to Black colleges. The media attention garnered by his enrollment helps to announce the excellent education that Foster is receiving at Southern to an audience that would likely learn of Southern's program for the first time. Additionally, Foster's admission was a case of the Southern faculty examining the accomplishments of the individual, rather than simply his LSAT score. The admissions committee considered Foster's previous record of accomplishment and determined that he would be a worthwhile addition to the Southern Law School. Perhaps most important, his reflections on his positive experiences as a student helps to educate the public that Black colleges provide an excellent education that takes into account work schedules and student potential.

In 1998, *Ebony* magazine featured an article discussing the experience of Steven Schukei, who at the time was a twenty-one-year-old senior at Morehouse College. Like Governor Foster, Schukei was a White male attending a historically Black college; however, his prominence came through his campus activities rather than his position outside of the university. With his election to the office of vice president of student government, Schukei became the first

White student to serve as an officer of the Morehouse student body (Chappell 1998). Schukei credited Morehouse for generating in him confidence and teaching him the importance of leadership:

> Morehouse does an excellent job of creating strong leaders. The way Morehouse does that is by giving students the courage and self-confidence to go on and do what they need to do. Schukei said, "I have confidence to do things, even though I might not be successful. Running for vice president, I didn't know whether I would win or not, but Morehouse gave me the confidence to do it anyway. . . . I have that confidence. It's part of the Morehouse Mystique. The Mystique is that and a whole lot more. It's something that's hard to define. It's having the confidence to do what you need to do, to stand for the things that need to be stood for and to live your life [in an] exemplary [way]." (qtd. in Chappell 1998, 64)

Schukei's experience at Morehouse is fully consistent with the ideals set forth by those who form the Morehouse legacy. In the words of Dr. Walter Massey, the College's president: "I think it says Morehouse students judge their classmates on the basis of the character and ability, which I'm very proud of. Steve seems to be a valued member of the Morehouse community. It's consistent with my vision, Dr. King's vision, as well as Benjamin Mays' vision" (qtd. in Chappell 1998, 64).

As Willie has remarked, there are numerous lessons that Schukei has had to learn as a member of a White minority group at Morehouse, and his public mastery of such lessons has proved inspirational to others, evidenced in the words of another White student at Morehouse: "I really look up to him. He has made it a lot easier for me and other White students to follow in his footsteps" (qtd. in Chappell 1998, 64). Like former U.S. Senator Harris Wofford, a Howard University graduate, one of the founders of the Peace Corps, and CEO of the Corporation for National Service, Schukei is gaining a valuable perspective in the historically Black college environment in which Whites are subdominant in power and number. Negotiating this environment has benefits for the individual, the institution, and society.


## CONCLUSION

What place do HBCUs occupy in the U.S. higher education landscape? In this chapter, the unique contributions made by these institutions have been highlighted: a unique educational and service purpose, a unique pedagogical and curricular focus, the mentoring approach of faculty in the education of students, and admissions that favor hard-working students with potential, whether these students have or have not been well served by the K–12 educational system.

Black colleges, born in the crucible of segregation in postbellum America, instantly faced challenges unique to other postsecondary institutions. Black colleges were valueless to Black Americans as way stations for privileged youth; these institutions initially had an absolute need to address the intellectual, practical, and spiritual needs of a people recently delivered from bondage. Among competing interests from Black religious leaders, captains of industry, and White missionaries, Black colleges eked out an existence that first improved the lives of everyday Black Americans—though the constituencies directing this effort were often at odds with one another and sometimes did not have the humanitarian interest of Black Americans in mind.

First, the fact that these institutions served a population previously excluded from formal education led leaders such as Booker T. Washington to focus on an immediate, practical education that could be applied to the everyday lives of African Americans. At the same time, W. E. B. Du Bois advocated that Black schools also serve the growing intellectual leadership of the African-American community. Rather than choosing a Washingtonian path over Du Bois's (or vice versa), Black colleges and universities synthesized both approaches because such an amalgamation was in the best interests of Black Americans. Through an approach that recognized the tragedy of Black education in America, HBCUs emphasized student potential over student performance, which likely was affected by a lack of facilities and funding in the elementary and secondary schools. Equally important, however, was the charge to students and graduates that the privilege of a college education was not a self-serving exercise; rather, it was a community-supported action that required service to the community in return. The legacy of African-American leaders in commerce and industry, in the arts and sciences, in the humanities, and in public service professions speaks to this mission at HBCUs.

The men and women who taught and continue to teach at HBCUs are presented with students who have the capacity to change their communities and society, with appropriate guidance. This understanding makes faculty at Black colleges particularly sensitive to the importance of developing students with great character as well as great minds. It is interesting to note in an era when predominantly White institutions (and the students and parents they serve) are focusing on factors such as student-teacher ratios, average test scores of the student body, and the proportion of applicants rejected, Black colleges serve as the exemplar that chooses to emphasize the future promise of students as well as past accomplishments.

In the postbellum era to the modern day, Black colleges have understood the inadequacy of educational opportunity not just for Blacks but for other groups in American society. Veterans, the working class, women, immigrants, the economically disadvantaged, and people of color are often not afforded the educational advantages that others in this nation have enjoyed. Hence, historically Black institutions have sought to fill their classrooms with capable students with a full understanding of this disparity. These college admissions decisions tend to emphasize indicators such as character, strong work ethic, and the ability to overcome obstacles—precisely the same criteria that many predominantly White private institutions (and large public institutions in the aftermath of affirmative action lawsuits) extol. Such a philosophy at the front door does not equate to mediocrity in educational attainment, however. These very same institutions have produced more professionals and leaders than one would expect and, in some instances, more Black students of high intellectual caliber than other types of institutions in the American higher education system. Rather than limiting this gift to Black Americans, an astonishingly diverse population of scholars could benefit from the focus on student potential and the emphasis on student development emphasized in HBCUs.

Today's discourse on Black colleges and universities rests in an interesting position. On one hand, HBCUs are enjoying a renaissance of sorts, with media personalities and national leaders supporting the work of these institutions. On the other hand, financial challenges, as well as enrollment and accreditation issues, plague many Black institutions. A legal climate that calls for HBCUs to justify their existence *without* recognizing the historical climate in which these institutions were formed also presents a worrying prognosis on the future of Black colleges and universities. Even when misunderstood by other colleagues in higher education, HBCUs continue to believe that they have a unique mission and a charge to keep. They continue to be inspired by the civil rights movement and its song "We Shall Overcome," and they do.

An appropriate conception of HBCUs grants them an important, pivotal place in American higher education. These are the institutions that educated well some students believed to be unfit for higher education. Black colleges have proven that good faculty support can prepare students for medical school and a successful career in other professions. They do this by introducing innovative approaches such as evening classes, remediation, and tutoring that are now embraced in higher education.

We believe that Black colleges still continue to contribute to the American landscape of higher education. Faculty diversity in gender, race, ethnicity, religion, and age are areas in which Black colleges and universities can offer lessons to other institutions that are uncertain about whether it is better to be inclusive or exclusive.

Given these facts, the case for the HBCUs seems evident. We are left to wonder why these facts are not known and why the value of these institutions is called into question. Willie and Hedgepeth present a compelling hypothesis of why this is so: "Because Blacks in the past have been so preoccupied with defending their right to exist, they have not been granted the privilege of fully explaining their educational goals so that others might understand and learn. This discussion is an effort in that direction, an explication of the norms that guide the educational experiences provided by predominantly Black colleges" (Willie and Hedgepeth 1979, 90).

This volume, then, is the latest effort to highlight the success of these institutions in bridging cultural knowledge, reversing the power dynamic among racial lines, and providing an environment where Blacks, as well as persons from all ethnic, cultural, and racial groups, can prosper. Such learning environments in HBCUs are described by Willie and Hedgepeth as schools that promote a double culture and a double consciousness (as articulated by Du Bois) and teach students how to achieve a double victory, as discussed in chapter 1.

*Part III*

# PERSONAL AND PROFESSIONAL CHARACTERISTICS OF PRESIDENTS OF HISTORICALLY BLACK COLLEGES AND UNIVERSITIES

*Chapter Five*

# Personal Characteristics, Professional Pathways, and Management Challenges of Presidents

## INTRODUCTION AND METHODOLOGY

Since the 1800s, historically Black colleges and universities (HBCUs) have been an important facet of the American higher education landscape. Like many higher education institutions, HBCUs have had to evolve and adapt to ever-changing social, political, and economic conditions of the nation. And, their leaders have also had to evolve and adapt. These leaders are expected to personify the unique educational missions and values of these institutions; they are looked to for intellectual leadership; they are responsible for the development of sound institutional policy; and they are expected to garner external support. The current chapter adds to the growing interest in HBCUs by focusing on their presidents and chief executive officers (CEOs).

Using a forty-question survey, in 2001 the American Council on Education (ACE) collected personal and professional information on the leaders of various types of American higher education institutions. The questionnaires were mailed to 3,848 presidents, CEOs, and system heads of institutions of higher education. Of that number, 2,594 presidents responded, yielding a response rate of 67 percent.

This chapter reanalyzes the ACE data for presidents of HBCUs. Of the total 2,594 responses received by ACE, 59 questionnaires were completed by leaders of HBCUs. Our study is limited to presidents of four-year colleges founded before 1964 that are nationally accredited and offer a baccalaureate

This chapter is based on a subset of the 2001 data compiled on college and university presidents by the American Council on Education. Permission to use and reanalyze these data are acknowledged with appreciation.

degree. Our sample consisted of 48 HBCUs evenly divided between public and private institutions.

The chapter is divided into three sections dealing with personal and professional lives of HBCU presidents. The first section, "Personal Characteristics of Presidents of Historically Black Colleges and Universities," reviews demographic information such as race, age, gender, marital status, number of children (if any), labor force status of spouse, and highest degree earned. The second section, "Career Paths of Presidents of Historically Black Colleges and Universities," reviews the available data pertaining to the presidents' manner of ascension to the institutional helm, including their age, length of service, the governance structure of the institutions they serve, and their work experience before becoming president. The third section, "Management Issues and Challenges of HBCU Presidents," reviews the data on administration matters that occupy much of the presidents' time and the issues they felt least prepared to confront.

## PERSONAL CHARACTERISTICS OF PRESIDENTS OF HISTORICALLY BLACK COLLEGES AND UNIVERSITIES

While several HBCUs had White presidents in past years, more than 97 percent of the contemporary presidents who responded to the questions about race and ethnicity identified themselves as African American; ten survey respondents did not answer this question (table 5.1). These data reveal that an overwhelming number of HBCU presidents today are Black. White leadership of HBCUs during the early days of these institutions has given way to Black leadership today in public as well as private institutions.

Not only are most HBCUs led by Black presidents, an increasing number of HBCU boards of trustees are chaired by Blacks as well, indicating an increasing appreciation of the leadership capacity of Black people. When White educator and philanthropist Charles Merrill decided to end his long tenure as the chair of the board of trustees at Morehouse College, he was pleased that the

**Table 5.1.   Race/ethnicity of presidents**

| Race/Ethnicity | Number | Percent |
|---|---|---|
| Black/African-American | 38 | 97 |
| White/Non-Hispanic | 1 | 3 |
| Total | 39* | 100 |

*n=sample of 48; no response from 9
*Source:* National President's Survey, American Council on Education (2001).

**Table 5.2.   Age range of presidents**

| Age Range | Number | Percent |
|-----------|--------|---------|
| 41–50 | 3 | 7 |
| 51–60 | 24 | 55 |
| 61–70 | 11 | 25 |
| 71+ | 6 | 14 |
| Total | 44* | 100 |

*n=sample of 48; no response from 4
*Source:* National President's Survey, American Council on Education (2001).

faculty and board were diversified. However, he said that it was time for the appointment of a Black chairperson as well.

Although Blacks have gained access to leadership positions within HBCU governance structures, the issue of race remains. With White students attending a few HBCUs in increasing numbers, there is concern that a large demographic shift in enrollment will lead to the displacement of Blacks in the administration. However, the present information does not confirm this concern. For example, Bowie State, Delaware State, Kentucky State, Langston University, and Lincoln University (Missouri), all known as HBCUs, had White students who represented 30 percent or more of their student bodies in 2002. Yet, the current presidents of all of these institutions are Black.

The modal age for presidents of HBCUs is the ten-year interval between fifty-one and sixty years of age (table 5.2). Fifty-five percent (a majority) of all HBCU presidents are found in this middle-age category. Less than one-tenth (7 percent) of the presidents ascend to the status of CEO before they turn fifty. This experience is similar to that for all presidents of colleges and universities in this nation (American Council on Education 2001, 50). However, 14 percent of HBCU presidents are seventy-one years of age or older and are still serving. This is a finding that is more or less unique to the leadership of Black colleges and universities.

While 80 percent of HBCU presidents are between fifty-one and seventy years old, as is true for all college presidents in America, we call attention to the fact that the proportion of HBCU leaders seventy-one years and older (14 percent) is twice the proportion of those under fifty years of age and is a proportion much larger than the 2 percent for all presidents in this upper age level in the United States (American Council on Education 2001, 50).

Why do Black colleges accommodate and retain older administrators? *A New Look at Black Families* by Willie and Reddick (2003) used the Typology of Modes of Group Adaptation developed by Robert Merton (Merton 1968, 126) that indicate group tendencies to conform to cultural norms or to be innovative.

When applying this mode to all families, we discovered that affluent Black families tended to be the most conformist of all family groups in this nation. They believe in democratic decision making and that the institutions of U.S. society should protect the weak from the strong (Willie and Reddick 2003, 13). These are central ideas in the American way of life. A universal characteristic of all Black families is their hope that their children will have a better life than the elders experienced. Because older Black educators in particular are permanent members of the "booster's" club for younger Black people, young Blacks have no need to turn away from the older generation. While some may classify the protective actions by older adults as "overprotection," still it is beneficial for young people to know that the elders are on their side and are cheerleaders for better life chances for them.

Thus, older people seem to be respected among Blacks not because of their age alone but because of the confidence that older people have in younger Black people. For this reason, younger Black people tend to trust their elders. Confidence and trust, when they happen simultaneously, result in mutual respect. We are reminded of how Benjamin Mays supported Martin Luther King Jr.'s position that he should return to Montgomery even though it was a certainty that he would be arrested for helping to organize the bus boycott for racial desegregation in 1956, as discussed in chapter 4.

This is an example of the significant supporting role of some older people who are presidents of Black colleges. Thus, we think that the enlarged number of Black college presidents over seventy years of age is neither an accident nor a chance occurrence. As said earlier, most younger Black people know that they can put their trust in older Black people and will not be disappointed. In the Black community there is much reciprocity between younger and older generations.

The gender makeup of our sample of HBCU presidents is overwhelmingly male (92 percent) (table 5.3). Obviously, there is greater access to the helms of these institutions for men than for women. This proportion for HBCU presidents is somewhat higher than the proportion of men (81 percent) who serve as college presidents in the nation as a whole. These and related issues will be discussed in greater detail in the next section.

Some of the nation's most prominent Black colleges—Fisk University, Bennett College, Johnson C. Smith University, Livingstone College, Norfolk State University, Spelman College, and Texas Southern University—are led by women. Though the number of HBCUs led by African-American women is few, the profiles and accomplishments of these CEOs are impressive. Beverly Daniel Tatum of Spelman and Johnetta Cole of Bennett came to the presidency from senior administrative positions at Mount Holyoke and Spelman, respectively. Both women are authors of considerable renown: Tatum's *Why*

**Table 5.3.**   **Gender of presidents**

| Gender | Number | Percent |
|--------|--------|---------|
| Male   | 44     | 92      |
| Female | 4      | 8       |
| Total  | 48     | 100     |

*Source:* National President's Survey, American Council on Education (2001).

*Are All the Black Kids Sitting Together in the Cafeteria? And Other Conversations about Race* (1997) is a best-selling psychology text, and Cole's *Conversations: Straight Talk with America's Sister President* (1993) gave readers an opportunity to hear from the woman responsible for garnering the largest single gift from individuals to any Black college—$20 million from Bill and Camille Cosby in 1987 (Bennett College 2004). These women are acclaimed scholars and administrators who are ably guiding these two private Black women's colleges into the twenty-first century.

Some women come to the presidency from outstanding careers in public service. Fisk University president Hazel O'Leary served as the secretary of energy under President Bill Clinton. Priscilla Dean Slade, who worked on Texas governor Rick Perry's gubernatorial transition team, leads the nation's largest HBCU, Texas Southern University. These leaders have demonstrated excellence in the public arena and bring such skills to the presidency of their institutions.

Perhaps most important, women HBCU presidents are role models and mentors to students and society. This generation of leaders is making a strong case for women as CEOs in higher education. It is important to note that women leaders have profound effects on men as well as women students. Nathan McCall, a professor at Emory University and author of the critically acclaimed *Makes Me Wanna Holler: A Young Black Man in America* (1994), credits Livingstone College president Algenia Freeman with helping him to turn his life around after he was incarcerated as a youth. His account of her mentorship is touching and compelling:

> [Dr. Algenia Freeman] was a former teacher of mine. I took a course under Dr. Freeman, and she took an interest in me. She invited me home for dinner. She understood that I was troubled and had issues, and she worked with me on that. . . . So we not only developed those relationships . . . we still maintain those relationships today. (McCall and Anderson 2002, 136)

The performance of Dr. Freeman demonstrates the educational value of women as presidents of HBCUs, and the fund-raising performance of Dr.

Johnetta Cole demonstrates the administrative value of women as presidents of HBCUs. As public servants, academics, role models, and mentors, women are becoming an emerging and powerful group of Black college CEOs. It is our belief that these pioneers are opening doors for more women to ascend to the presidency.

Marriage tends to be an important factor in the lives of college and university presidents that is reflected in these data (table 5.4). Eighty-eight percent of the respondents in the sample were married at the time of the survey, a percentage that is fairly consistent with that reflected by the overall ACE statistics (86 percent). Only 2 percent reported their marital status as divorced, compared with 6 percent for college/university presidents in the nation as a whole. The remaining 10 percent of HBCU presidents were either widowed or never married. Presidents who are currently married and those who are widowed or divorced represent 98 percent of all HBCU presidents. Ninety-seven percent of the respondents have children (table 5.5).

Almost two-thirds of the spouses of presidents are in the labor force, a fact that challenges traditional assumptions regarding the role of the spouse as a stay-at-home partner in the presidency (table 5.6). The fact that many spouses have independent employment signals a change in the spousal role of the CEO of educational institutions. This is a trend that should be watched carefully and studied in-depth to determine its meaning for all college and university presidents and the institutions they serve.

**Table 5.4.  Marital status of presidents**

| Marital Status | Number | Percent |
|---|---|---|
| Never Married | 1 | 2 |
| Married | 42 | 88 |
| Divorced | 1 | 2 |
| Widow/widower | 4 | 8 |
| Total | 48 | 100 |

*Source:* National President's Survey, American Council on Education (2001).

**Table 5.5.  Children in family of presidents**

| Children | Number | Percent |
|---|---|---|
| Yes | 28 | 97 |
| No | 1 | 3 |
| Total | 29* | 100 |

*n=sample of 48; no response from 9
*Source:* National President's Survey, American Council on Education (2001).

**Table 5.6.    Participation of spouse in labor force**

| Does Spouse Work? | Number | Percent |
|---|---|---|
| "Yes, in same institution" | 9 | 20 |
| "Yes, in different organization or institution" | 19 | 43 |
| No | 16 | 36 |
| Total | 44* | 100 |

*n=sample of 48; no response from 4
*Source:* National President's Survey, American Council on Education (2001).

**Table 5.7.    Highest degree earned by presidents**

| Highest Degree | Number | Percent |
|---|---|---|
| Doctorate (PhD, EdD, MD, JD) | 37 | 93 |
| Master's, other | 3 | 7 |
| Total | 40* | 100 |

*n=sample of 48; no response from 8
*Source:* National President's Survey, American Council on Education (2001).

The presidents of HBCUs in this sample are quite an accomplished group in terms of educational attainment (table 5.7). Ninety-three percent have a terminal doctoral degree—PhD, EdD, JD, or MD. This figure is comparable to the national statistics for degree attained by the presidents of all institutions and is noteworthy since most of the institutions in our sample are four-year colleges granting baccalaureate degrees. The leaders of the HBCUs today are well educated.

Notably, many HBCU presidents boast of educational credentials beyond the formal baccalaureate and doctorate degrees. Several presidents continue to participate in continuing education and professional development programs after their formal education. And many have been honored by their peers in higher education with honorary degrees and by the National Association for the Advancement of Colored People (NAACP) and the National Urban League, and they participate in graduate chapters of social organizations such as fraternities and sororities and in other organizations committed to uplifting the status of people of color.

## CAREER PATHS OF PRESIDENTS OF HISTORICALLY BLACK COLLEGES AND UNIVERSITIES

Despite longevity in office of a few presidents, about three-quarters of contemporary HBCU CEOs have served ten years or less, as seen in table 5.8.

Some of the more senior presidents mentioned earlier have served sixteen or more years; but they represent a small proportion of HBCU presidents.

We cannot determine from the data why HBCUs extend the term of president for some of its elders beyond the age of seventy. We do know that some presidents with long terms of service have made wonderful contributions to their schools. Again, we reference President Norman Francis and the achievements of his seasoned leadership at Xavier University. "Within the last five years," according to the Xavier University 2000–2002 catalog, this school "has awarded more undergraduate physical science degrees and placed more African Americans into medical school than any other college in the United States."

A similar record of great leadership was displayed by Benjamin Elijah Mays. He was president of Morehouse College for twenty-seven years and retired at age seventy-two, "after being persuaded by the faculty, alumni and trustees to stay on for two additional years beyond the mandatory retirement age" (Colston 2002, 163). Some of May's protégés called him "a student[-oriented] president" (167).

In recent years, however, rapid turnovers in the office of president have occurred at Fisk University, Paul Quinn College, Wiley College, Morris Brown College, and a few public institutions such as Grambling and Alabama A&M. Such rapid changes in institutional leadership are a threat to long-term planning, and this is a matter that has implications for the governing board and how it functions.

Most chief executive officers of colleges and universities are under contract and serve at the pleasure of the governing board. As seen in table 5.9, the governing board is the authority to which most presidents (81 percent) of Black higher educational institutions report. In this respect, the governing authority to which most HBCU presidents report is similar to the authority in charge of 75 percent of all colleges and universities in the United States (American Council on Education 2001, 51). This fact means that new presidents should

**Table 5.8.   Number of years current HBCU presidents have been in office**

| Years in Current Office | Number | Percent |
|---|---|---|
| 1 to 5 | 12 | 32 |
| 6 to 10 | 15 | 41 |
| 11 to 15 | 6 | 16 |
| 16 or more | 4 | 11 |
| Total | 37* | 100 |

*n=sample of 48; no response from 11
*Source:* National President's Survey, American Council on Education (2001).

receive a thorough orientation in president-board responsibilities and relationships and continuing education regarding these matters.

Most HBCU presidents, like presidents of other higher educational institutions (American Council on Education 2001, 52), are under contract as the chief administrative officer and are without the protection of a joint appointment to a tenured faculty position, as seen in table 5.10. This is the experience of 57 percent of HBCU top executives and 69 percent of all top executives in higher education in this nation. Clearly, presidents are expected to deliver for their institutions or suffer the consequences. Most of them do not have the additional security of a tenured faculty position.

Data presented in table 5.8 also reveal that nearly three-quarters (73 percent) of HBCU presidents have been in office ten years or less. This pattern of service of a decade or less is similar to the pattern of service found among all presidents (American Council of Education 2001, 52). Since this is not a longitudinal study, we do not know whether recently appointed presidents will have more or less than ten years of service at the same school. We suspect, however, that the cross-sectional data are rough indicators of length of service for most presidents and that a majority will remain in office less than ten years. This means that governing boards must consider what is the minimum term of office that is acceptable for both short-term and long-term planning; what responsibility, if any, the governing board has for both long-term and short-term tenure of the CEOs; and whether the recruiting practices of governing boards are finding the most able, effective, and compatible leaders (table 5.11).

**Table 5.9.  Person or organization to whom HBCU presidents report**

| Authority to Whom President Reports | Number | Percent |
| --- | --- | --- |
| Governing board | 38 | 81 |
| System head | 7 | 15 |
| Other | 2 | 4 |
| Total | 47* | 100 |

*n=sample of 48; no response from 1
*Source:* National President's Survey, American Council on Education (2001).

**Table 5.10.  HBCU presidents with or without tenure**

| Status | Number | Percent |
| --- | --- | --- |
| With tenure | 20 | 43 |
| Without tenure | 27 | 57 |
| Total | 47* | 100 |

*n=sample of 48; no response from 1
*Source:* National President's Survey, American Council on Education (2001).

**Table 5.11.   HBCU presidents who have served as CEO before current appointment**

| Previous Service as College or University CEO | Number | Percent |
|---|---|---|
| Never served as CEO before current appointment | 24 | 65 |
| Served as CEO once before current appointment | 10 | 27 |
| Served as CEO twice before current appointment | 3 | 8 |
| Total | 37* | 100 |

*n=sample of 48; no response from 11
*Source:* National President's Survey, American Council on Education (2001).

There is a limited practice of shifting and recycling college and university presidents from one school to another school. About one out of every three current HBCU presidents (29 percent) had been president elsewhere before assuming one's present responsibility (table 5.12). Although appointment as president is a new experience for most CEOs of HBCUs, nine out of every ten were associated with higher education institutions before becoming a college or university president. Only 10 percent of HBCU presidents moved into the presidential suite without any work experience on a college campus. Dr. Hazel O'Leary of Fisk University is one such person; her background is in science, politics, banking, and consulting, especially with reference to energy matters.

Moreover, at the college and university campuses where most presidents receive their on-the-job training in higher education administration, a large proportion (40 percent) were provost, dean of an academic division, or chair of an academic department. The proportion of presidents who made it to the top through the academic route (40 percent) was almost twice as great as the proportion of presidents whose previous experience as higher education administrators was in finance, development, external relations, or student affairs. These experiences for HBCU leaders are similar to the stepping stones

**Table 5.12.   Jobs held by HBCU presidents before current appointment**

| Previous Appointment before Current Job as President of a Higher Education Institution | Number | Percent |
|---|---|---|
| College or university president | 14 | 29 |
| "Senior administrator: provost, leader of academic division or department" | 19 | 40 |
| "Senior administrator: leader in finance, development, external or student affairs" | 9 | 21 |
| Employment outside of higher education | 5 | 10 |
| Total | 47* | 100 |

*n=sample of 48; no response from 1
*Source:* National President's Survey, American Council on Education (2001).

taken to the presidency by other CEOs of schools: 45 percent had appointments as academic administrators, and only 15 percent were employed outside higher education (American Council on Education 2001, 53).

The fact that so many HBCUs are led by former deans, professors, and administrators speaks to the fact that the pathway to the presidency parallels that of virtually all other institutions of higher education in this country. A few HBCUs will, however, appoint presidents who have demonstrated leadership in other arenas.

At some institutions, the practice of appointing former presidents of other institutions to lead HBCUs is indicative of the importance these institutions place on previous experience as a leader. In the case of Bennett College, Dr. Johnetta Cole had experience as Spelman College's first female president, and her expertise in development made her an ideal choice to lead another women's college with the need to successfully ensure its financial future. Dr. Henry Ponder, former president of Benedict College and of Fisk University as well as Alpha Phi Alpha Fraternity, Inc., and the National Association for Equal Opportunity in Higher Education (NAFEO), brought significant leadership experiences to the helm of Talladega College, which was in danger of losing its accreditation before his arrival. In his years as president, Ponder has helped the institution to successfully retain its accreditation. Spelman College looked to one of the foremost scholars in the area of race relations and psychology to assume leadership in naming Dr. Beverly Daniel Tatum president in 2002. Dr. Tatum previously served with distinction as a senior administrator at Mount Holyoke College, also a women's college.

Data in table 5.13 clearly reveal that most colleges and universities do not appoint their CEOs from within. Nearly eight of every ten new HBCU presidents (79 percent) worked for an institution other than the one over which they currently preside. A majority of all higher education institutions in the nation select their president from other institutions. In general, about six out of every ten new presidents (63 percent) of all colleges and universities came from a different institution than the one over which he or she currently presides (American Council on Education 2001, 53).

Promotions to the presidency from within, though rare, do occur on occasion. For example, Neari Warner had held numerous vice presidential positions spanning more than three decades at Grambling State University prior to her appointment as that university's president. Similarly, Robert Moore rose through the ranks of Bluefield State University, serving as division chair, assistant dean, and vice president over a span of sixteen years before his appointment as president in 1993.

With many years of work experience in higher education, some administrators have broadened their work experience, if only for a few years, in

**Table 5.13.    Institution of employment of HBCU presidents before current job**

| Institution of Employment before Current Job as President | Number | Percent |
|---|---|---|
| Same as institution of current employment | 8 | 21 |
| Different institution of employment | 31 | 79 |
| Total | 39* | 100 |

*n=sample of 48; no response from 9
*Source:* National President's Survey, American Council on Education (2001).

organizations other than those dedicated to education. As seen in table 5.14, nearly two-thirds (62 percent) have been employed elsewhere. However, only about one-quarter (26 percent) worked outside higher education more than five years. We cannot determine from the available data how the limited exposure of HBCU presidents to organizations and agencies that are not concerned with the production and distribution of knowledge has broadened their perspective on management.

Most individuals with experience in institutions other than higher education have been employed by governmental agencies and organizations in the not-for-profit sector. Few have been entrepreneurs in the business sectors. Examples of contemporary or recently retired Black college and university presidents with appointments in federal government are Walter Massey, president of Morehouse College; Louis Sullivan, former president of Morehouse Medical School; Walter Broadnax, president of Clark Atlanta University; Charles Hines, president of Prairie View A&M University; and Hazel O'Leary, president of Fisk University. Massey was director of the U.S. National Science Foundation; Sullivan was secretary of the U.S. Department of Health and Human Services; Broadnax was deputy secretary of the U.S. Department of Health and Human Services; Hines was a commissioned officer for thirty years and rose to the rank of major general in the U.S. Army; and O'Leary was secretary of the U.S. Department of Energy.

Another group of contemporary or recently retired HBCU presidents who, in the past, were employed in the not-for-profit sector are CEOs such as Benjamin Payton, president of Tuskegee University; Samuel D. Cook, retired president of Dillard University; and Robert M. Franklin, former president of the Interdenomination Theological Center. All three of these individuals have served as program officers of the Ford Foundation. In addition, Payton served as director of the Commission on Religion and Race and the Department of Social Justice of the National Council of Churches.

As mentioned above, few HBCU presidents have been connected with the business sector before their appointment. Michael Lomax, also a former president of Dillard and now president and CEO of the United Negro College

**Table 5.14.**    **Employment experience of HBCU presidents inside and outside of higher education during career**

| Years Employment Experience Outside Higher Education | Number | Percent |
|---|---|---|
| None | 14 | 36 |
| 1 to 5 | 14 | 36 |
| 6 to 10 | 7 | 16 |
| 11 or more | 4 | 10 |
| Total | 39* | 100 |

*n=sample of 48; no response from 9
*Source:* National President's Survey, American Council on Education (2001).

Fund, was an educator, elected official, and entrepreneur before becoming a college president. Lomax was elected to the Fulton County Board of Commissioners and served fourteen years, twelve as president. Fulton County is a civil district in Georgia that includes the City of Atlanta. An HBCU president with a strong connection to business is William Harvey. In addition to serving as president of Hampton University, Harvey is the owner of a Pepsi-Cola Bottling Company in Horton, Michigan.

HBCU presidents have had experiences in and outside the academy that are similar to those of all presidents of higher education institutions. Thirty-one percent of CEOs of all colleges and universities in this nation have been employed outside higher education for more than five years (American Council on Education 2002, 67).

Finally, we are interested in determining whether the presidency in HBCUs and in traditionally White institutions (TWIs) is open with parity to women as well as men. The answer, regretfully, is no. Ninety-two percent of the presidents in our sample of HBCUs are male and only 8 percent are female, as seen in table 5.3. Thus, less than one out of every ten HBCU presidents is a woman. For the nation as a whole the record is slightly better, with women being about two out of every ten presidents (American Council on Education 2002, 63). Both proportions indicate that much work is needed to redistribute authority and responsibility among men and women with parity in higher education administration, especially since women represent the largest proportion of students in colleges and universities pursuing baccalaureate and master's degrees today.

A study by Andrew Hacker found that "90 percent of men who head colleges are married" but that only "57 percent of women college presidents are married" (Hacker 2003, B11). Although the number of women in our sample is small, the marital status of female presidents of HBCUs is similar to findings in the Hacker study. Clearly, the proportion of nonmarried women leaders in higher education administration is significantly less than the proportion of non-married men among Blacks as well as Whites. More research is needed to determine why this fact has not changed over the years.

## MANAGEMENT ISSUES AND CHALLENGES
## OF HBCU PRESIDENTS

In general, matters related to money are among the great challenges facing institutions of higher education today. HBCUs are no exception and, in fact, appear to be severely affected in a negative way by financial matters. Cross and Slater (1994) provide statistics that highlight the dismal state of financial resources of HBCUs in comparison to TWIs. "The combined endowment of all forty-one private black colleges represented by the UNCF (United Negro College Fund) is less than the endowment of . . . Swarthmore College in Pennsylvania" (Cross and Slater 1994, 76). Inadequate resources is a common experience of many HBCUs.

The typical HBCU president is challenged by fiscal issues and spends much of his or her time dealing with these. Budgeting, fund-raising, and strategic planning seem to combine and emerge as a central thematic issue for HBCU presidents. As seen in table 5.15, 38 percent of the presidents reported that they were insufficiently prepared for effective fund-raising; 33 percent were insufficiently prepared for strategic planning; and financial management was reported by 27 percent of HBCU presidents as an area in which they were insufficiently prepared. These are self-reported data that may or may not be

Table 5.15.   **In which of the following areas did you feel insufficiently prepared?**

| Area | Full sample (%) | Publics (%) | Privates (%) |
|------|-----------------|-------------|--------------|
| Academic program management | 10 | 4 | 17 |
| Collective bargaining | 21 | 21 | 21 |
| Conflict management | 19 | 21 | 17 |
| Crisis management | 15 | 8 | 21 |
| Federal/state policy issues | 19 | 4 | 33 |
| Financial management | 27 | 29 | 25 |
| Fundraising | 38 | 38 | 38 |
| Intercollegiate athletics | 30 | 29 | 29 |
| Personnel issues | 6 | 4 | 8 |
| Public relations | 6 | 0 | 13 |
| Strategic planning | 33 | 29 | 38 |
| Student life issues | 13 | 8 | 17 |

*Source:* National President's Survey, American Council on Education (2001).
*Note:* The sample size is 48.

objective. Nevertheless, they give us an indication of perceived challenges that HBCU presidents face.

## Fund-raising

Few institutions charge tuitions that are high enough to cover all costs of a student's education. Various financial aid strategies are used to make higher education available to students in a wide range of economic categories. These strategies—such as scholarships, grants, and work/study projects—further drive up expenses for the institutions that provide them and require continuous fund-raising to cover a school's budget. While 38 percent of the respondents reported insufficient preparation in the area of fund-raising, we note that this large proportion is less than a majority. However, possessing fund-raising skills is of limited value if people in the donor pool are not able or inclined to be generous to requests for help from HBCUs.

Some HBCUs have done exceedingly well in the area of fund-raising. Hampton University under the leadership of Dr. William Harvey, Morehouse College led by Dr. Walter Massey, and Spelman College formerly led by Dr. Johnetta Cole are examples of institutions and their leaders who have raised significant amounts of capital to strengthen their schools. These institutions are among the elite in the HBCU category and have very few peers in the area of fund-raising. Even though collaborative organizations such as the United Negro College Fund and the Thurgood Marshall Scholarship Fund have been successful, they do not meet the full and extraordinary financial needs of Black colleges and universities. Since most of the CEOs of HBCUs ascended to the presidency via an academic route, as mentioned earlier, it is probable that they may need assistance in methods and techniques of fund-raising and in other fiscal matters. From the data available, we cannot determine which presidents had prior experience in the area of fund-raising. However, it is conceivable that many have not had the fund-raising experience needed for success as an HBCU president.

## Strategic Planning

Strategic planning, a closely related activity to fund-raising, was also identified as an area of challenge by one-third (33 percent) of respondents in the ACE survey of presidents. Such planning involves identifying institutional goals and aligning them with fund-raising strategies to implement them. Strategic planning is institution-specific and must take into consideration the community and social context within which a higher education institution exists. Few HBCU graduates have obtained during the course of adulthood

sufficient income to be genuine philanthropists who can give the funds necessary to implement strategic plans for their institutions. Vernon Clement Jones
reported that "an average of only 5 percent to 10 percent of alumni [among
black schools] made annual gifts, compared with an average of about 25 percent [of alumni] for all private schools" (Jones 2003).

## Financial Management/Budget

The financial constraints characteristic of many HBCUs demand careful
budgetary and financial management by their presidents. A fourth (27 percent)
of respondents reported feeling insufficiently prepared for this role. With
increasing reliance on resources from governmental agencies, budget control
mechanisms are essential. Governmental resources have been withdrawn
from a few HBCUs because of inadequate accounting procedures. Table 5.15
indicates that private HBCUs, in particular, have presidents who feel they are
insufficiently prepared to deal with federal/state policy issues. The proportion
of private HBCU presidents with this feeling is 33 percent, placing this matter in the top three for which they feel insufficiently prepared. As seen in table
5.15, federal/state policy issues is not a category that is bothersome to presidents of public HBCUs, probably because they have to deal with state agencies frequently.

The fiscal theme arises again when respondents were asked to identify the
top four areas that occupy significant amounts of their time. As shown in table
5.16, sixty percent of the presidents reported that they spent much time with
budgetary matters. Additionally, more than half of the respondents (56 percent) identified fund-raising as an area that required much of their attention.
Almost half (46 percent) of the respondents selected planning as an activity
exerting significant demands on their time. Thus, budget, fund-raising, and
strategic planning were areas in which HBCU presidents felt insufficiently
prepared and were also areas that occupied most of their time. It is probable
that enhancing the competency of HBCU presidents to deal with fiscal matters
may free up more time to deal with persisting educational problems.

Taken together, the data in tables 5.15 and 5.16 indicate differences, if any,
between the responses of presidents of public and private institutions. Fed-
eral/state policy issues and relations with legislators emerged as matters in
which responses differed for leaders of public and private institutions. As
stated earlier, 33 percent of the presidents of private institutions reported feeling insufficiently prepared in the area of federal/state policy issues, however,
only 4 percent of the presidents at public institutions reported insufficient
preparation in this area. This perhaps reflects the greater degree to which leaders of public institutions must interact with governmental agencies because

**Table 5.16.  Top four areas that occupy the most significant amount of your time**

| Area | Full sample (%) | Publics (%) | Privates (%) |
|---|---|---|---|
| Academic issues | 35 | 29 | 42 |
| Athletics | 0 | 0 | 0 |
| Board relations | 19 | 13 | 25 |
| Budget | 60 | 58 | 63 |
| Community relations | 13 | 17 | 8 |
| Fund-raising | 56 | 46 | 67 |
| Personnel issues | 27 | 25 | 29 |
| Planning | 46 | 38 | 54 |
| Relations with legislators and political officials | 15 | 29 | 0 |
| Student issues | 25 | 21 | 29 |

*Source:* National President's Survey, American Council on Education (2001).
*Note:* The sample size is 48.

they receive most of their funding from these sources. Also, none of the presidents of private institutions identified relations with legislators and political officials as one of the top four areas that occupy a significant amount of their time. Conversely, 29 percent of the leaders of public institutions reported that relations with legislators and political officials occupied a significant amount of time. In short, leaders of private institutions reported less preparation for and least day-to-day involvement in federal, state, or local governmental matters than leaders of public institutions.

Private and public HBCUs were similar in that budget and fund-raising were the top two matters that captured most of the time of their presidents (table 5.17). The amount of time given to budget matters of 58 percent and 63 percent, respectively, for public and private HBCUs was similar. But the amount of time that private HBCU presidents allotted to fund-raising (67 percent) was much greater than the 46 percent allotted to the same activity by public HBCU presidents.

Providing for the fiscal health of an institution draws the president away from more traditional academic functions such as research and teaching. Slightly less than half the respondents (48 percent) reported writing for a scholarly publication during the period of their presidency, and slightly more than one-third (38 percent) of HBCU presidents taught a course alone or in a team-teaching arrangement. A very small proportion of HBCU presidents (14 percent) were personally engaged in research. Apparently, fiscal matters along with the other demands of the presidency are so time-consuming that they cancel out opportunities to participation in educational activity other than administration. Although most HBCU presidents came to this office from the

**Table 5.17.   Academic activities performed by presidents**

| Academic Area | Number | Percent Yes | Percent No | Total |
|---|---|---|---|---|
| Teach a course by yourself | 3 | 10 | 90 | 48 |
| Team teach a course | 8 | 28 | 72 | 48 |
| Write for scholarly publication | 14 | 48 | 52 | 48 |
| Conduct research | 4 | 14 | 86 | 48 |

*Source:* National President's Survey, American Council on Education (2001).

academic side of the institution, most higher education administrators no longer have time to pursue their scholarly interests. Thus, higher education administration may be identified as a sacrificial effort for academically oriented presidents.

## CONCLUSION

This study has revealed that 90 percent of HBCU presidents identify themselves as Black. These school leaders have education and other qualifications similar to those of all presidents of higher education institutions in the United States. This is a cause for celebration. But this wonderful achievement could become a double-edged sword in that these presidents are eligible for employment elsewhere. This reality means that governance boards for HBCUs must give more attention to ways of supporting their CEOs to prevent losing them, since they are now part of the national market of executive talent.

In general, HBCUs tend to select men between fifty and sixty years of age to be their CEOs. In this respect, their practice is similar to that of all institutions in the nation. They differ from other institutions, however, in that they also engage the services of a small but significant number of presidents who are seventy years of age and older.

Available data are insufficient to determine whether some older administrators are retained because of their wisdom or because the pool of candidates from which to choose a successor is so small that schools are unwilling to take a chance on a new executive if they can retain the older executive of proven ability. There is a possibility that HBCUs are culturally inclined to honor older people. However, evidence to prove or disprove this conjecture is unavailable. Examples of presidents with long-term service, such as Benjamin Mays and Norman Francis, reveal without doubt that the accomplishments of some older executives have been and are extraordinary. And these older presidents have demonstrated that they have confidence in younger people and are willing to mentor them.

While age seems not be an impediment for hiring and retaining a president at HBCUs, gender does seem to be a barrier. Despite the fact that more women than men matriculate in baccalaureate and master's degree programs in HBCUs as well as in colleges and universities throughout the nation, women range from one-tenth to one-fifth of the presidents of colleges and universities in the 2001 sample of the ACE study. Although a few women, such as Dr. Ruth Simmons of Brown University and Dr. Mary Sue Coleman of the University of Michigan, have salaries in "the Half-Million Club" (Basinger 2002) and have achieved parity with salaries of men who assume similar responsibilities, women presidents of HBCUs and other colleges and universities in the United States are still underrepresented. In the ACE study, only about one out of every ten presidents of an HBCU and only about two out of every ten presidents of other higher education institutions were women.

Although education is an institution in our society that is related to all other institutions, it also is relatively autonomous. Thus, higher education, including HBCUs and other schools, tend to recruit their highest executive officer from among scholars who have had administrative experience in academic affairs in colleges and universities. Few schools appoint presidents from faculty or administrators who already work at the college or university seeking a new leader. Some institutions, including HBCUs, are not reluctant to call a president who has been president of another institution. Nevertheless, most presidents tend to be newcomers to the office, serving for the first time as a CEO of a college or university. The fact that most presidents come up through academic ranks indicates that intensive briefings in nonacademic areas such as finance, development, and external relations may be needed, especially for neophytes.

While HBCUs may differ from other schools in several ways, their presidents and their ascendancy to the helm are similar to the pathway of ascendancy of other chief executives in education. Thus, the knowledge and skills needed by HBCU leaders, as was shown in this study, are similar to the knowledge and skills needed by all higher education leaders. However, HBCUs may have unique needs requiring skills that differ from those required by other presidents because of the limited income of families from which many of their students come, the absence of very wealthy alumni, inadequate endowment funds, and the continuing effects of racial discrimination in the United States.

*Part IV*

# SUMMARY AND
# ACTION STRATEGIES

# Chapter Six

# Black Colleges Redefined

## *A Summary*

The minority is a curious reflection of the majority. We say curious because in the human social system the minority provides a double reflection: It indicates what the society has been and what it could be. Richard Wright recognized this several decades ago when he wrote, "We Black folk, our history and our present being, are a mirror of all the manifold experiences of America" (Wright and Rosskam 1941, 146). Whites, he said, can better understand themselves as the majority by coming to know minorities.

We begin this discussion by emphasizing the function of minorities in society with the hope that this analysis will replace the frame of reference used by present and past national leaders such as Daniel Patrick Moynihan. He suggested that progress of the minority is seriously retarded when its way of life "is out of line with the rest of American society" (U.S. Department of Labor 1965, 29). This statement implies that mainstream behavior is that exhibited by Whites and that behavior of minorities should be imitative of the majority, that they should be remade in the image of Whites. And Christopher Jencks and David Riesman, in a 1967 *Harvard Educational Review* article, "The American Negro College," called the Black college of mid-twentieth century "an ill-financed, ill-staffed caricature of White higher education" (Jencks and Riesman 1967, 24).

Michael Meyers has attempted to dismiss the argument for the continuation of Black colleges as an "outcry of emotionalism, ethnic chauvinism, and paternalism." He summed up his view with this statement: "No matter what else is taught or how well it is taught, the fact that a school is segregated teaches that there is a qualitative difference between students in Black and [in] White colleges" (qtd. in Willie 1979, 46). Clearly Meyer's assumption is that Black colleges are second rate.

Apparently, any approach to education that differs for Blacks does not make sense to Meyers or Moynihan. In this respect, they are ideological bedfellows. The logic of positing a different educational approach for the minority is lost by both critics. Meyers has formulated the question wrongly in assuming that "the issue at stake in the current controversy over all-Black colleges is segregation" (qtd. in Willie 1979, 46). Others believe that the issue is education!

With this kind of criticism coming from the friends of Black institutions, it is difficult for these colleges and universities to get a hearing regarding what they can, could, and should do not only for Blacks but for the education of the nation. Our national history offers evidence that the approach of the minority may in the end be of great value to the majority. W. E. B. Du Bois said that the public school system in most southern states began with the enfranchisement of Blacks. The idea that the masses should be educated to effectively participate in public decision making was formulated by Thomas Jefferson several decades before the Civil War but was not implemented until Blacks became members of southern state legislatures during Reconstruction. In the early years of the nineteenth century, there was no public educational system in the South, except perhaps in North Carolina. In his study *Black Reconstruction in America,* Du Bois said that education was regarded by poor Whites before the Civil War "as a luxury connected with wealth" (Du Bois 1962, 641). In Thomas Jefferson's Virginia, for example, "less than one-half of poor White children were attending any school" (639). The laws passed in South Carolina between 1856 and 1870 that authorized tax-supported schools open to all were described as "the most beneficial legislation the state . . . has ever enacted." These laws were initiated and supported by elected Black lawmakers during the Reconstruction era, according to research findings of Du Bois (648–650).

One could say of Reconstruction Black legislators that former slaves and the progeny of former slaves fulfilled for all people the slave owner's dream of publicly supported education in the South. In contemporary times, Blacks have continued to link legislation and the idea of liberation in a way that has improved education for members of their own race and for Whites. Each day Allan Bakke, who is White, should thank God that there are racial minorities in America whose political action resulted in a law that prohibited racial discrimination in employment and that guaranteed his right to attend the medical school of his choice. That law is the Civil Rights Act of 1964, which Bakke invoked to gain admission to the Davis Campus Medical School of the University of California (Sindler 1978).

John Monro (1978) has said, as mentioned earlier, that if more White colleges used readings from Black authors, readings that develop a full and accurate awareness of the American Black experience, this country would be much better off. We also believed that research projects on methods and techniques of effective teaching in Black colleges would result in a valuable contribution from the Black experience. The findings of such studies could benefit all colleges— selective as well as open-door institutions. Daniel Thompson, former provost and vice president of Dillard University, told the Black College Conference at Harvard that "the work of talented, dedicated, persevering teachers has substantiated the claim of Black colleges that they can take certain students who are rejected by most or all of the affluent, high ranking, prestigious White colleges and produce a relatively large proportion of topflight college graduates." This can be done, Thompson pointed out, because "teachers in Black colleges . . . are more concerned with classroom activities, personal counseling, sponsoring organizations." He described the interaction between students and teachers at Black colleges as "many sided, sustained and personal." The top faculty members often teach lower-division students because "they want to lay as solid a foundation as possible at the start of the college career so that academic development will be sound and continuous" (Thompson 1978, 180–194).

Some policy makers and educators have seized on this asset of Black colleges—the extraordinary attention given to students, including remedial courses offered if necessary—and have tried by way of reductionism to turn it into a liability. They have suggested that the future of higher education would be served best if most Black colleges became two-year institutions. This assertion fails to recognize the multiple goals that these colleges fulfill.

Black colleges and universities have kept alive interest in the pursuit of honesty, justice, and altruism in higher education. They have helped the nation recognize the difference between information and knowledge, on the one hand, and knowledge and wisdom, on the other. W. B. Schrader, in a College Entrance Examination Board study, reported the findings of Junius Davis on the qualities college teachers value in students (Schrader 1971, 119). In addition to intellectual quickness, creativity, and motivation to achieve, the teachers valued honesty, open-mindedness, pleasantness, self-understanding, and altruism (Davis 1965, 15–18). Black colleges and universities have emphasized the five values mentioned above as well as academic courses.

The former president of Harvard University and other White academic leaders had to wrestle with the moral and ethical issues arising from their institutions' investments in corporations that transacted business in South Africa during the era of apartheid (Anon. 1978, 77–78). After a great deal of soul searching, Derek Bok, then president of Harvard, said,

> Injustice and suffering are plainly matters of grave concern. We may justly feel impelled to give our time and effort as individuals to the struggle against these evils. We may also expect the university not to act deliberately to increase the suffering of others. But the principal issue before us is whether we should go further

and use the university as a means of expressing moral disapproval or as a weapon in our fight against injustice even if we threaten to injure the academic functions of the institution. . . . Universities are designed to achieve particular purposes. Their special mission is the discovery and transmission of knowledge. . . . Their institutional goal is not to reform society in specific ways. Universities have neither the mandate nor the competence to administer foreign policy, set our social and economic priorities, enforce standards of conduct in the society, or carry out other social functions apart from learning and discovery. (Harvard College statement, qtd. in Willie 1981a, 145–153)

Moreover, the Harvard president asserted, "We should also recognize that very rarely will the institutional acts of a single university—or even universities as a group—have any substantial possibility of putting an end to the misfortunes that exist in society" (Harvard College statement, qtd. in Willie 1981a, 107).

Back in 1945, when Martin Luther King Jr. was completing his first year at Morehouse College, the president of that school said in a radio address, "It will not be sufficient for Morehouse College . . . to produce clever graduates, men fluent in speech and able to argue their way through; but rather honest men, men who are sensitive to the wrongs, the sufferings, and the injustices of society and who are willing to accept responsibility for correcting the ills" (qtd. in Bennett 1977, 78). Ten years later during the Montgomery bus boycott, King acted out the words he had heard from his college president, Benjamin Mays.

Note that the White school president, Derek Bok, emphasized the *analysis* function of higher education institutions while the Black school president, Benjamin Mays, emphasized the *action* function of higher education institutions. Clearly, analysis and action complement each other; one without the other is incomplete. Thus, our nation needs predominantly White and predominantly Black educational institutions to give due emphasis to both functions.

Historian L. D. Reddick described Morehouse College as a place where "teachers encouraged their students to explore and search for solutions to campus and world problems," a place where "nobody on the faculty seemed to be afraid to think and speak out," a place where the president "was willing to be counted" (Reddick 1959, 68). King's dedication to social justice was bound up with his Morehouse College education. Black colleges have been concerned with group advancement as well as individual success, and they have placed greater emphasis on participation in the processes of democracy than have most White institutions. There is no paradox in this; those who are denied the rights of democratic citizenship are likely to value them more highly than those who can take them for granted.

Gregory Kannerstein, who studied the self-concepts of several Black colleges, concluded that "perhaps the greatest and most distinctive contribution of Black colleges to the American philosophy of higher education has been to emphasize and legitimate public and community service as a major objective of colleges and universities." Kannerstein said that statements of the purpose of most Black colleges reveal a "litany of 'education-citizenship-leadership-democracy' that affirms a belief in the democratic process and in the ability of colleges, students, and alumni to influence it" (Kannerstein 1978, 31).

While the Black college that King attended emphasized service and citizenship, it also provided him with a good academic education. In fact, a significant percentage of its baccalaureates have earned doctorate degrees. Thus, a focus on service and citizenship need not result in neglect of academic goals. Most Black colleges strive to provide their students with a comprehensive education having to do with excellence as well as equity.

Black colleges are also flexible enough to combine classical and career education at a time when a growing number of White as well as Black students are insisting that college should equip them with sufficient skills to get a good job after graduation. This synthesis of liberal arts and vocationally oriented courses first emerged in Black colleges and universities and placed these institutions in the vanguard of higher education; it grew out of the Booker T. Washington-W. E. B. Du Bois debate at the beginning of the twentieth century on the nature of higher education appropriate for Blacks. At that time, the discussion was ignored as merely a fuss between two Blacks. But by the time of the turbulent 1960s, White colleges realized that teaching students how to survive and to do things with their heart, head, and hands was as important as teaching and learning in the liberal arts tradition.

Approximately 15 percent of the total number of students attending historically Black public colleges are classified as non-Black. Black colleges, though they were segregated by law, have never been segregating institutions; they have always had a substantial number of White faculty members. HBCUs could and should teach other institutions how to become pluralistic in their teaching staff.

Social science studies have revealed that in order to make an educational impact and to negotiate effectively with students and teachers, racial minority students should constitute about 20 percent of a school's student body. Black colleges that have White enrollments of 15 percent or more are within striking distance of this goal of one-fifth of the student body for a White or non-Black minority. The ideal minimum for a single racial or ethnic minority group or a combination of such groups is a population of at least one-third that differs from the predominant group.

Thus, one possible future function for Black colleges is that of serving as settings in which Whites may enroll and experience the beneficial effects of being a minority group. There is nothing intrinsically good about being the majority, and there is nothing intrinsically bad about being the minority. In a pluralistic and cosmopolitan society, everyone may be part of a minority in one context or another at some time. So it is well that, in school, Whites should learn not to fear the consequences of minority status, and people of color should learn to be comfortable with the responsibilities of majority status. Empathy is a frequent outcome of minority status that all should have the privilege of learning. Empathy, of course, is a form of behavior not limited to minority status. But people in such a category seem to have more opportunities to practice empathy, an important emotional intelligence. For this reason, all should have the privilege of experiencing minority status.

This idea grew out of the experience of a court-appointed panel in the Boston school desegregation cases *Morgan et al. v. Hennigan et al.* (1974) and *Morgan v. Kerrigan* (1975). The senior author was a court-appointed master to help develop a desegregation plan. The plan recommended that student bodies should be diversified rather than strictly balanced. In other words, some schools could have a majority of Whites in the student body and a sufficient minority of Black and Brown students to have educational impact on the total system. Other schools could have a majority of Black and Brown students with a sufficient minority of Whites to have a meaningful influence. This proposal for elementary and secondary public schools is certainly appropriate for public and private colleges. Whites can experience minority status only if there are predominantly Black or Brown institutions in which to enroll. Thus, the retention of predominantly Black colleges and universities is for the benefit of the total society, including Whites as well as Blacks.

In the past, Black legislators helped to enrich the nation by supporting the development of a state systems of public education. Moreover, state-supported as well as private Black colleges have been pioneers among other community institutions in demonstrating how to integrate disparate adult population groups, especially faculties. Similar ingenuity could be used to desegregate all college and university student bodies. To do this, Black colleges and universities must refuse to cooperate in their own oppression by eliminating their historic identity, and they should never try to be exclusive. A self-centered attempt to save Black institutions for Blacks only would be as damaging as trying to remake them in the image of White institutions. Both actions ultimately would end in defeat. Black colleges and universities must be preserved for the value they add to society as a whole. A higher educational system that has a Harvard but not a Hampton is incomplete. Thus, Black colleges and universities have a *future* in our society because of their unique *function.*

*Chapter Seven*

# Action Strategies for Presidents and Boards

Based on the findings in this study, the following recommendations are suggested for chief administrators and boards to ensure the vitality and sustainability of historically Black colleges and universities (HBCUs) in the twenty-first century.

## REAFFIRM DIVERSITY AND INCLUSION INITIATIVES

HBCUs have emphasized over the years that the practice of segregating based on race, ethnicity, and other characteristics has no place in admissions policies of education institutions. In the past, HBCUs accepted all kinds of people and educated them well in diversified student bodies—diversified in terms of previous educational experiences, learning styles, preparation for college studies, religion, and socioeconomic status.

Most HBCUs are reluctant to classify themselves as "open-door" institutions; nevertheless, some are. And most of these schools have a stellar record of turning many disadvantaged and underprepared students with many learning deficiencies into excellent scholars who have made valuable contributions to the communities in which they live and to society at large.

HBCUs rejected "the [nineteenth century] idea of competition, natural selection, and the survival of the fittest" that, according to E. F. Schumacher, has dominated the minds of educated people today (Schumacher 1973, 88). Sarah Willie's study of Black graduates of Howard University found that "positive support from faculty clearly gave the men and women . . . a sense that they were a group" (Willie 2003, 85). And effective groups support and sustain their members. In *The Multicultural Student's Guide to Colleges*,

Robert Mitchell reports that "the Morehouse [College] faculty . . . is as supportive of students as students are of one another. Many give students their home telephone numbers." Said one student, "The professors here want to see you do well. . . . Everyone here, from professors to other students, wants you to succeed. In other words, there's little cut throat competition" (Mitchell 1993, 188).

These values facilitate the accommodation of students with a range of talents. As the population of this nation becomes increasingly pluralistic and multicultural, other schools could learn from HBCUs how to effectively manage diversity in a learning environment. All institutions, and particularly higher education institutions, should learn how to do this because, we are bold to assert, diversity will be a major challenge of the twenty-first century. We are not alone in making this assertion. *American Diversity: A Demographic Challenge* is the title of a book recently published by Mary Denton and Steward Tolney, who state that "nowhere is this trend more prominent than on college campuses" (Denton and Tolney 2002, 1).

Because Black colleges and universities have been leaders in creating racial and ethnic diversity among faculty and gender and socioeconomic diversity among students and have welcomed to their campuses individuals with a variety of learning styles and precollege preparation, they are uniquely positioned to help higher education embrace and not be afraid of the future challenge of diversity. By reclaiming diversity and inclusion as important components of the mission of higher education, HBCUs may teach through precept and example effective ways of reconciling pluralistic population groups into an interdependent and cooperative learning community.

An excellent example of the benefits derived from diversity is the Morehouse College experience. When the head of the Georgia State NAACP asked Benjamin Mays, the president of Morehouse College, if Horace Ward would be a good candidate to integrate the law school student body of the University of Georgia in the 1950s, Mays immediately gave his heartfelt approval. Ward was a 1949 graduate of Morehouse College with a good record (Mays 1971, 205–206), but the law school at the University of Georgia would not accept him as a student then.

Hamilton Holmes, who had spent only two semesters and three months at Morehouse in 1959, was urged by Mays and others to seek admission to the University of Georgia as an undergraduate during the 1960–1961 school year. Mays said, "I wanted to see the racial barriers at the University broken down, and I wanted a Morehouse student to be the first [Black] male to do it" (Mays 1971, 208).

Mays kept in close touch with Holmes during his three years at the University of Georgia. Having learned of the high quality of Holmes's work during the first quarter, Mays "challenged him to make Phi Beta Kappa" (Mays 1971, 208). Holmes met the challenge and was initiated in this society of scholars during his senior year at the University of Georgia.

Challenging the White South and proving that segregation was unacceptable, Mays felt responsible to do whatever he could to integrate other schools in Georgia as well as the school over which he presided, especially its faculty. Mays said that the competition for Black scholars was "terrific." For "this . . . reason," he said, "I sought to secure faculty members beyond the [Black] community. . . . Today the Morehouse faculty has Jews, [Blacks], Protestants, Catholics, Hindus, Africans, white southerners and white northerners. We sought to hire men and women of high academic achievement and good character, teachers who had risen above prejudice" (Mays 1971, 178–179). And, of course, the students have benefited from instruction received from a diversified faculty.

Mays also was able to recruit to the Morehouse Board of Trustees in 1954 a White educator and philanthropist, Charles E. Merrill Jr., who became chair of the board in 1959 and remained chair beyond the retirement of President Mays in 1967. Edward A. Jones, who wrote a history of Morehouse College, reported that Morehouse was fortunate in having as its chair of the board "a man . . . [who] understands the major problems of Morehouse and has addressed himself to their solution." Jones said that Merrill "acquir[ed] . . . firsthand knowledge of what goes on in the classroom" and elsewhere (Jones 1967, 191).

In the president's 1958 annual report, Mays said that "Morehouse must do everything it can to assist its students to overcome the handicaps of the past [and] to prepare them to meet the competition of a desegregated society." President Mays declared that "More effective teaching . . . must be our constant aim" (Mays, qtd. in Jones 1967, 176) and that "a college is no stronger than its faculty" (Mays 1971, 278).

Jones reported that "when Harvard's president Nathan Pusey visited the Morehouse campus in June 1962 to deliver the commencement address, he marveled at the number of Morehouse seniors who had been admitted to well-known graduate schools with generous scholarships, fellowships, and assistantships" (Jones 1967, 172).

Clearly, a diversified teaching staff has been value added to the education of Morehouse students and students in other Black schools. Information about this proven outcome of diversity should be shared with other schools. Morehouse College assembled a multicultural faculty that was concerned with teaching students as well as subjects.

Since Morehouse College and other Black colleges helped integrate White schools by urging some of their best students to seek enrollment during the time of the civil rights movement, now is the time for reciprocity (Becker 1980). Whites should reciprocate by urging some of their students to enroll in predominantly Black schools. As mentioned in chapter 4, a few White students already have benefited from such an experience.

Substantial faculty diversity in many traditionally White institutions (TWIs) remains a goal yet to be attained. Thus, HBCUs must continue to demonstrate in their schools the benefits of diversity in faculty, staff, and governing boards and how to achieve such diversity.

## CULTIVATE MULTIPLE INTELLIGENCES

Several years ago, sociologist Daniel Bell declared that "the post-industrial society . . . is a meritocracy. . . . [I]n the nature of meritocracy . . . what is central to the assessment of a person is the assumed relation of achievement to intelligence." Asserting that the number of talented persons in a society as measured by IQ is a limited pool, Bell stated that "by the logic of meritocracy, these high scoring individuals, no matter where they are in society, should be brought to the top in order to make the best use of their talents" (Bell 1997, 607–608).

Black colleges and universities have overwhelming evidence that leadership should not be restricted to high-scoring individuals on standardized tests or any other ranking system. A decade after the death of Martin Luther King Jr., Hugh Gloster, then president of Morehouse College, said that Dr. King was "the archetype of an educated person—one who combined academic achievement and professional success with personal integrity and social concern." He said the life of Martin Luther King Jr. was worthy of emulation by all (Morehouse College 1980, 5).

King was a graduate of Morehouse College, an HBCU. When he graduated, he had a grade point average of 2.5, which is halfway between B and C. The believers in meritocracy would not have brought him to the top. Yet, this magnificent leader of the civil rights movement was called "a saint" by former Morehouse College Board of Trustees chair Charles Merrill and "a prophet" by former Morehouse College president Benjamin Mays because of his extraordinary commitment, skill, and accomplishments. Dr. Mays, in the eulogy at King's funeral, said that this leader "gave people an ethical and moral way to engage in activities designed to perfect social change without bloodshed and violence" (Mays 1969, 13, 10). At Crozier Theological Seminary, Martin Luther King Jr. received a grade of C in public speaking. At Bates College, Benjamin Mays received a grade of D in one of his language courses. Yet, these two men became two of the best orators and scholars in the United States.

To summarize, HBCUs know that effective leadership is concerned with both equity and excellence, that one without the other is incomplete. One may sharpen a personal talent by pursuing procedures that generate excellence. However, the achievement of equity has to do with fairness in the distribution of goods, opportunities and services among a collectivity of people. High scorers on intelligence or aptitude tests may not indicate that such individuals also have learned how to be fair. We ignore at our peril a basic responsibility of higher education to teach all of us how to be just, equitable, and fair. From the Black experience in America, HBCUs have learned that "love is the boss principle in life," that "justice is love distributed" (Fletcher 1966, 69, 80, 87), and also that justice is fairness (Rawls 2001).

## REAFFIRM CONFIDENCE, TRUST, AND RESPECT AS ESSENTIAL COMPONENTS OF EDUCATION

Higher education institutions have grown accustomed to the practice of putting students on trial and working with them only if they prove that they are worthy. This practice ignores the responsibility of the dominant people of power (teachers and administrators) to show confidence in students who are uncertain of their talent and their capacity to achieve. Some people perform well because others believe in them. The annals of HBCUs are filled with personal stories of students (such as Dr. James A. Hefner, an economist and former president of Tennessee State University) who were given a chance and who bloomed into good scholars because of the confidence their teachers had in them (Hefner 2000, 10–11).

The beginning of formal education at the college level for most Black people in the United States came after the Civil War. Although a majority of Blacks had no formal education, the founders of schools for Black students believed that if given the opportunity the former slaves would overcome their learning deficits. And they did. Approximately a century and one-third later, Norman Francis, president of Xavier University, a predominantly Black school in New Orleans, Louisiana, expressed a similar attitude about some of its students: "Where others say, 'they're not going to make it,' we say, 'we think they can.' And we give them a chance" (qtd. in Cose 1997, 53). The chance that HBCUs give to underachievers as determined by standardized tests represents the confidence these schools and their teachers have in their students, which in turn contributes to a relationship of trust among students for their teachers. And these relationships of confidence and trust generate mutual respect. For these reasons we call confidence, trust, and respect essential actions in formal education (Willie 2000, 262). It should go without saying that confidence, trust, and respect are important in all learning environments. HBCUs have brought this important message to our attention. Our contemporary experience demonstrates that some of the standard indicators of academic promise are false positives. While women had lower average scores than men on both the verbal and the mathematical sections of the SAT (in 2001), a higher proportion of women than men had grade-point averages in the A and B ranges (in 2000). With grade-point averages in the C and D range (in 2000), the proportion of men exceeded the proportion of women with lower grades. When SAT scores in verbal and mathematical sections are combined, Asians had higher average scores than Whites. But a higher proportion of White students than Asian students had grade-point averages in the A range (in 2000) (Anon. 2003, 12). There is inconsistency in the measurement of effectiveness by the indicators mentioned above.

Because of these and other inconsistencies, HBCUs use a variety of indicators of academic performance and academic promise. As stated earlier by one HBCU president, his college "succeed[s] in reopening doors which have been closed to many students whose potentials have been judged by instruments developed for the majority culture" (Willie and MacLeish 1978, 138). HBCUs consider honesty, altruism, empathy, and fairness as indicators of academic success as well as the development of language and computing skills.

## CONTINUE TO FOSTER EMPATHY AND OPPORTUNITIES FOR MULTICULTURAL RELATIONS

Because of their multicultural faculty, HBCUs have provided opportunities for many White professors to develop a deep and abiding empathy for people of color. Archetypical examples of such people discussed in this study are John Monro, who taught English composition and literature at Miles College and Tougaloo College, and Theodore Currier, who taught history at Fisk University. These White professors loved and respected their students and had confidence in their capacity to perform well if given the chance. An indication of the depth of their empathy was their readiness to serve, sacrifice for, and suffer with their students.

These multicultural encounters are mutually beneficial for faculty and students in that the White faculty members learn to be compassionate by exhibiting confidence in their students, and the students learn that there are White people who can be trusted. HBCUs have done a marvelous job of creating readiness in Black and in White faculty members and among students of color for the approaching age of diversity in our local communities and in our global economy. Missing from this equation is the cultivation of White students who need to learn how to be courageous and live successfully as a minority person in a new, diversified society. HBCUs have achieved meaningful diversity at the faculty level. White institutions could learn from their achievement and do likewise. More studies on how HBCUs have operated effectively for many years with diversified faculties are needed so that other institutions can learn from their experience.

## ENHANCE THE STRUCTURE AND FUNCTION OF ADMINISTRATIVE SERVICES

There is considerable interest in staff development for administrators at HBCUs. Our study of a sample of forty-eight CEOs, half presiding over private schools and half presiding over public schools, indicates that the ascendancy path to the office of president at HBCUs is not much different from the ascendancy path of most presidents of higher education institutions in the United States. With reference to education and other qualifications, CEOs in HBCUs have achieved parity with other higher education presidents. What is different for administrators of HBCUs is their lack of access to economic resources that are sufficient for the needs of the institutions they operate.

In the mid-1970s, Charles Willie and Marlene MacLeish conducted a study of seventeen public and private HBCUs and discovered that "Although committed to educat[ing] any and all who are willing to work diligently for a college [degree,] presidents of Black colleges . . . must give as much attention to refurbishing or expanding the physical plant and to finding funds for student aid, faculty salaries, library and teaching materials as to other educational matters" (Willie and MacLeish 1978, 141). Thus, presidents of HBCUs confront circumstances somewhat different from the circumstances that other presidents confront because of their small endowments, limited income of their students' families, and, consequently, the lower tuition they tend to charge.

Our current study discovered that these problems continued to confront HBCU presidents today. The top two areas that occupy most of the time of CEOs of HBCUs are budget (indicated by 60 percent) and fund-raising (indicated by 56 percent). And one of the top two areas in which CEOs of HBCUs felt insufficiently prepared was fund-raising (indicated by 38 percent). Clearly, matters of fund-raising and financial management (budget making and control) are common experiences for most HBCU presidents that are troublesome. Consequently, HBCU boards must be attentive to these pressures and exercise leadership to solve these institutional challenges for and with their CEOs.

We believe that financial matters are troublesome experiences for many HBCU presidents and boards for two reasons. Most of the current CEOs ascended to the rank of president through academic offices such as provost, dean of an academic division, or chair of an academic department. Less than one-fifth became president after serving as a higher education leader in finance or development. And as stated earlier, pricing tuition and room and board at the same rate charged by most schools in the United States is not an option for HBCUs because of the precarious economic circumstances of many of their students.

While academic programs, student affairs, personnel issues, and public relations are important items on a CEO's agenda, they were not major problems for the HBCU presidents in this study. The prevailing problems had to do with financial matters and issues such as accreditation, academic program development, and faculty hiring and retention. These are major concerns on which presidents as well as boards should work together.

The HBCU presidents have great expectations for their schools. However, a generation ago they reported in the survey conducted by Willie and MacLeish that "35–40 percent of the priorities [they had for their schools] depend[ed] on resources external to their institutions. . . . About half of these priorities dealt with educational matters such as curriculum reform, faculty development, improving the system for advising students, innovations in [the curriculum], including the design of new graduate programs and undergraduate concentrations in the professions" (Willie and MacLeish 1978, 141). The realization of these goals require substantial and sustainable financial resources.

Since the income of Black households was only 61 percent of that for Whites a generation ago, HBCU presidents concluded that external resources are necessary for the innovations they would like to introduce. This circumstance continues until today; the median income for Black households in the year 2000 had inched up to only 64 percent of Whites, which means that HBCU presidents must continue to raise funds from sources other than students and their parents. This is the reason that much of their time is consumed with fund-raising. Boards should play a crucial role in linking their institutions to external sources of financial support so that the fund-raising responsibility is shared by the board as well as the president.

The data available to us did not indicate whether or not the governing board of colleges and universities to which most of the presidents report understand this catch-22 situation of education planning versus fund-raising in which CEOs of HBCUs are caught. If board members do not understand the financial and educational pressures the CEO confronts, then board development as well as professional development for CEOs regarding financial matters may be necessary and essential.

Effective and committed leadership at all levels will be essential for the future vitality and sustainability of HBCUs. It will be critical for boards of trustees of HBCUs to support, enhance, and develop leadership throughout the institutions they oversee and guide. In particular, boards should attempt to identify and support leadership development efforts not only for HBCU presidents and the senior leadership teams but also for other HBCU leaders (deans, department chairs, and staff directors). Over the long term, boards should continue to be aware of the pipeline for future senior leadership of HBCUs and seek ways to expand and sustain it. In doing so, the HBCU sector in higher education will be strengthened.

Finally, it is important for HBCU boards themselves to think about their own leadership development in much the same way. One contribution to board reform may be the introduction of term limits for trustees. Also, the boundaries between policy making and policy implementation should be reviewed periodically so that board members and higher education administrators are mutually aware of their different as well as their similar responsibilities. And, of course, boards as well as the senior administrative team should develop a planning process that will promote stability in policies that help everyone and change in policies that harm anyone in the academic community. Identifying and supporting new trustees and identifying and expanding the pipeline for future board members will also be important ways of strengthening the HBCU sector.

## CONTINUE TO EMPHASIZE MENTORING AS AN IMPORTANT COMPONENT OF TEACHING

Several examples of mentoring have been mentioned in this book. Black colleges seem to recognize that young people need help in sorting out the various aspects of their lives. Some of their teachers have carried out mentoring in extraordinary ways. Perhaps the best way to underscore why mentoring should continue to be emphasized is to provide a short discussion on how good mentoring benefited the senior author of this book. Charles Willie tells us about the mentoring he received at Morehouse College, which was similar to the mentoring John Hope Franklin received at Fisk University and James Hefner received at North Carolina A. and T. State University, as undergraduate students. The schools mentioned above are HBCUs.

In college, I majored in sociology. During my senior year, Professor Walter Chivers, the chair of the Department of Sociology at Morehouse College in Atlanta, Georgia, took a special interest in me and my career. He advised me to enroll in Atlanta University immediately after graduating from college to study for a Master of Arts degree in sociology.

After I won a tuition scholarship from Atlanta University, Professor Chivers approached the president of Morehouse College, Dr. Benjamin Mays, and convinced him to establish a teaching assistantship in the Department of Sociology of my undergraduate school. There was only one candidate for this position. It was me. The salary for my work that year was not negotiated; it was exactly the cost of room and board at Atlanta University, the school of my matriculation for the master's degree. I remember well the experience of picking up my check monthly from the business office of Morehouse College, signing it, and turning it over immediately to the bursar at Atlanta University. The job of teaching assistant was created especially for me. I was probably the first teaching assistant Professor Chivers ever had in the Department of Sociology. Dr. Mays, the president of my undergraduate school, was an accomplice in this arrangement. As president of the sophomore, junior, and senior class and editor of the student paper, *The Maroon Tiger,* I knew that I was one of the president's favorite students because of the leadership responsibilities I assumed on campus. However, my grade point average when I graduated from college was good but not great.

My sociology professor mentor at Morehouse had other plans for his protégé after Atlanta University studies. Believing that I should continue graduate education for a doctoral degree, Professor Chivers again convinced the president of my undergraduate school to provide him with sufficient resources to invite to the Morehouse College campus a guest lecturer, the chair of the Department of Sociology at Syracuse University, whom he met and befriended at a national sociology meeting. The strategy of my mentor was to bring the Syracuse University professor to Morehouse College and introduce his protégé to him. His strategy had an effective outcome.

Honestly, I cannot remember the topic of the Syracuse professor's lecture. However, I do remember that before he left the Morehouse campus, he had promised to intercede in my behalf with the Syracuse University Department of Sociology and urge it to grant a scholarship to me if I applied and was admitted to the PhD program in the graduate school.

After completing my master's degree, it was my intention to seek employment probably in a social service agency such as the YMCA. But my mentor believed that I had another calling. I trusted his judgment, left the South, and traveled to New York State to enroll in Syracuse University—a region far removed from my Dallas hometown in spatial and cultural ways.

Syracuse University and I were a good match. I received a PhD degree in sociology in 1957, eight years after enrolling in 1949. I served Syracuse University as a teaching assistant, faculty member, chair of the Department of Sociology, and finally vice president for Student Affairs. Later, Syracuse awarded me an honorary doctorate degree and also gave me its highest alumni award three and one-half decades after I earned my terminal degree. All of this, directly and indirectly, may be attributed to the efforts of my mentors, especially Professor Walter Chivers and President Benjamin Mays, who acted in my behalf to facilitate the continuation of my formal education after college.

The former chair of the Board of Trustees of Morehouse College, Charles Merrill, said in 1976 at a Black College Conference at Harvard that Dr. Mays gave an almost religious value to the PhD degree, which probably more Morehouse graduates had earned during the years of this presidency than graduates of any other college. In addition to establishing high standards for students at Morehouse College, administrators and faculty members provided sufficient mentoring to help students reach these standards. The June 24, 2004, electronic *JBHE Weekly Bulletin* indicates why Elizabeth City State University graduates 54 percent of all students who enroll in this school. It achieves this goal that is 15 percentage points higher than the national average for African Americans by pursuing another form of mentoring. "It is not uncommon for a professor to call up a student in his or her dorm room to compel [one] to get out of bed and come to class" (Anon. 2004, 4). This and other examples of mentoring mentioned above enable HBCUs to enhance the education of some students whom other schools would reject. These are effective educational methods and techniques developed by HBCUs that should be examined and used by TWIs and other institutions of higher education for the benefit of all students.

# References

Allen, W. 1992. "The Color of Success: African-American College Student Outcomes at Predominantly White and Historically Black Public Colleges and Universities." *Harvard Educational Review* 62(1): 26–44.

Allen W., and J. Jewell. 2002. "A Backward Glance Forward: Past, Present, and Future Perspectives on Historically Black Colleges and Universities." *Review of Higher Education* 25(3): 241–261.

American Council on Education. 2001. *The American College President.* Washington, DC: ACE Fulfillment Service.

———. 2002. *The American College President.* Washington, DC: ACE Fulfillment Service.

Anderson, J. 1988. *The Education of Blacks in the South, 1860–1935.* Chapel Hill: University of North Carolina Press.

Anon. 1998. "More White Students are Attending Black Colleges, Officials Say." *Jet,* July 20, p. 26.

———. 1978. "South African Investments: A Vexing Problem?" *Harvard Magazine* 80(6) (July/August): 77–78.

———. 2000a. "Faculty Demographics." *Black Issues in Higher Education,* November 23, p. 32.

———. 2000b. "White Students Outnumber Blacks at Some of Nation's Historically Black Colleges." *Jet,* February 28, p. 31.

———. 2003. "Average SAT Scores" and "Undergraduate Grade-Point Averages." *Chronicle of Higher Education* 50(1) (August 29): 12.

———. 2004. *JBHE Weekly Bulletin,* June 24, p. 4, http://www.jbhe.com.

Baron, J., and M. Norman. 1992. "SATs, Achievement Tests, and High-School Class Rank as Predictors of College Performance." *Educational and Psychological Measurement* 52: 1047–1055.

Basinger, J. 2002. "The Growing $500,000 Club: 27 Private-College Presidents Earned More Than Half a Million in Compensation in 2000–1." *Chronicle of Higher Education* 49(1) (November 22): A1, A30–A33.

Becker, Lawrence. 1980. *Reciprocity.* Chicago, IL: University of Chicago Press.

Bell, Daniel. 1973. "On Meritocracy and Equality." In *Power and Ideology in Education,* ed. Jerome Krabel and A. H. Halsey, 607–635. New York: Oxford University Press.

Bennett, L. 1977. "Benjamin E. Mays: The Last of the Great School Masters." *Ebony* 33 (December), p. 78.

Bennett College. 2004. "Johnetta B. Cole Names 19th President of Bennett College." Bennett College press release, http://www.bennett.edu/jbe/jbcrelease.htm (accessed August 5, 2004).

BES (Barron's Educational Series). 1994. *Barron's Profiles of American Colleges,* 20th ed. Hauppauge, NY: College Division of Barron's Educational Series.

Black Excel. 2002. *The Black Excel Newsletter.* May 2002, http://www.blackexcel.org/may-2002.htm (accessed July 6, 2003).

Blackwell, J. 1976. *Black Colleges as a National Resource: Beyond 1975.* Atlanta: Southern Education Foundation.

Bowen, W., and D. Bok. 1998. *The Shape of the River: Long-term Consequences of Considering Race in College and University Admissions.* Princeton, NJ: Princeton University Press.

Brown, M., and K. Freeman. 2002. "Guest Editor's Introduction." *Review of Higher Education* 25: 237–239.

Buber, Martin. 1951. *Two Types of Faith.* New York: Macmillan. (Harper Torchbook edition published in 1961.)

———. 1955. *Between Man and Man.* Boston, MA: Beacon.

Burd, S. 1995. "Remarkable Rise of Clark Atlanta." *Chronicle of Higher Education,* March 24, http://chronicle.com/prm/che-data/articles.dir/articles-41.dir/issue-28.dir/28a02901.htm (accessed September 4, 2003).

Carter-Williams, M. 1984. "Student Enrollment Trends in Black Colleges: Past, Current, and Future Perspectives." In *Black Colleges and Universities: Challenges for the Future,* ed. A. Garibaldi, 219–245. New York: Praeger.

Cecelski, D. 1994. *Along Freedom Road: Hyde County, North Carolina, and the Fate of Black Schools in the South.* Chapel Hill: University of North Carolina Press.

Chappell, K. 1998. "Reverse Integration: White Student Blends in a Black College." *Ebony,* May, p. 64.

CHE. 2003. *The Chronicle of Higher Education: Almanac Issue.* Vol. 50, No. 1 (August 29). Washington, DC: Chronicle of Higher Education.

Cole, J. 1993. *Conversations: Straight Talk with America's Sister President.* New York: Doubleday.

Coleman, J. S. 1968. "Equality of Educational Opportunity." *Integrated Education* 6(5): (Sept./Oct.), p. 25.

Colston, Freddie C., ed. 2002. *Dr. Benjamin E. Mays Speaks.* Lanham, MD: University Press of America.

Cook, S. D. 1978. "The Socio-Ethical Role: Responsibility of Black College Graduates." In *Black Colleges in America: Challenge, Development, Survival,* ed. C. Willie and R. Edmonds, 51–57. New York: Teachers College Press.

Cose, E. 1997. *Color-Blind: Seeing beyond Race in a Race-Obsessed World.* New York: HarperCollins.

Cross, T., and R. B. Slater. 1994. "The Financial Footings of the Black Colleges." *Journal of Blacks in Higher Education* 6: 76–69.

Davis, J. 1965. "What College Teachers Value in Students." *College Board Review* 56, pp. 15–18.

DEBA (Division of Economics and Business Administration). 2003. *Course Descriptions.* Atlanta, GA: Morehouse College. http://www.morehouse.edu/busecon/bus.coursedescriptions.html (accessed September 4, 2003).

Delaney P. 1998. "The Whitening of our Black State Colleges." *Essence,* May, p. 226.

Denton, Nancy A., and S. E. Tolney, eds. 2002. *American Diversity: A Demographic Challenge.* Albany: State University of New York Press.

Drewry, Henry, and Humphrey Doerman. 2001. *Stand and Prosper: Private Black Colleges and Their Students.* Princeton, NJ: Princeton University Press.

Du Bois, W. E. B. 1903. *The Souls of Black Folk.* Chicago, IL: A. C. McClung; reprint, New York: Dover Publications, 1994.

——— 1962. *Black Reconstruction in America.* New York: Russell & Russell.

———. 1904. "The Talented Tenth." In *The Black American,* ed. Leslie H. Fishel and Benjamin Quarles, 226–228. Glenview, WI: Scott Foresman (published in 1970).

Dyer, S. 2001. "Law School a Learning Experience for Louisiana Governor." *Black Issues in Higher Education,* January 4, p. 26.

———. 2003. "Southern Law Center's Increasing White Enrollment Concerns Lawmaker." *Black Issues in Higher Education,* June 19, p. 9.

Ellison, Ralph W. 1952. *Invisible Man.* New York: Random House.

Fields, D. 2000. "Can HBCUs Compete for Black Faculty? Black Colleges Are Searching for Ways to Draw Top Talent." *Black Issues in Higher Education,* November 23, p. 32.

Flacks, R., and S. L. Thomas. 1998. "Among Affluent Students, a Culture of Disengagement." *Chronicle of Higher Education,* November 27, A48.

Fletcher, Joseph. 1966. *Situation Ethics.* Philadelphia, PA: Westminster.

Foster, Lenoar. 2001. "The Not-So-Invisible Professors: White Faculty at the Black College." *Urban Education* 36(5) (November): 611–629.

Foster, Lenoar, J. A. Guyden, and A. L. Miller, eds. 1999. *Affirmed Action: Essays on the Academic and Social Lives of White Faculty Members at Historically Black Colleges and Universities.* Lanham, MD: Rowman and Littlefield.

Frederick, D. Patterson Research Institute. 1997. *The African American Education Data Book.* Fairfax, VA: United Negro College Fund.

Hacker, Andrew. 2003. "How the B.A. Gap Widens the Chasm between Men and Women." *Chronicle of Higher Education,* June 20, p. B10–B11.

Hazzard, T. 1988. *Attitudes and Perceptions of White Students Attending Historically Black Colleges and Universities.* Doctoral research paper, Florida State University.

Hedgepeth, C., R. Edmonds, and A. Craig. 1978. "Overview." In *Black Colleges in America: Challenge, Development, Survival,* ed. C. Willie and R. Edmonds, 17–28. New York: Teachers College Press.

Hefner, Jame A. 2000. "The Challenges of Liberal Arts at a State Institution: A President's Perspective." *The Boulé Journal*, Winter, pp. 10–12.

Hoffer, Eric. 1951. *The True Believer.* New York: Harper Perennial.

Hrabowski, F. 2002. "The Living Legacy of Historically Black Colleges and Universities." *Black Issues in Higher Education,* July 18, p. 35.

Jackson, John H. 2001. *The Effects of the Racial Composition of an Institution on College Choice and Desegregation.* EdD dissertation, Harvard University.

Jencks, C., and D. Riesman. 1967. "The American Negro College." *Harvard Educational Review* 37(1) (Summer/Fall): 3–60.

Jerome, Judson. 1971. *Culture Out of Anarchy.* New York: Herder and Herder.

Jewell, Joseph O. 2002. "To Set an Example: The Tradition of Diversity at Historically Black Colleges and Universities." *Urban Education* 37(1) (January): 7–21.

Johnson, Tobe. 1971. "The Black College System." *Daedalus* 100: 798–812.

Jones, Ann. 1973. *Uncle Tom's Campus.* New York: Praeger.

Jones, Edward A. 1967. *A Candle in the Dark: A History of Morehouse College.* Valley Forge, PA: Judson Press.

Jones, Vernon Clement. 2003. "The Call To Give Back." *Wall Street Journal,* September 17.

Jost, Kenneth. 2003. "Black Colleges: Issues." *CQ Researcher* 13(43) (December 12): 1045–1068.

Kannerstein, G. 1978. "Black Colleges: Self-Concept." In *Black Colleges in America: Challenge, Development, Survival,* ed. C. Willie and R. Edmonds, 29–50. New York: Teachers College Press.

King, Martin Luther, Jr. 1958. *Stride Toward Freedom.* New York: Harper and Row.

———. 1968a. *The Drum Major Instinct.* Atlanta: The Estate of Martin Luther King Jr., http://www.stanford.edu/group/King/publictions/sermons/680204.000_Drum_Major_Instinct.html (accessed September 19, 2005).

———. 1968b. *Where Do We Go from Here: Chaos or Community.* New York: Bantam.

Kushner, Harold S. 1981. *When Bad Things Happen to Good People.* New York: Schocken Books.

Levinson, A. 2000. "As Different as Day and Night: Missouri's Historically Black Lincoln University, Now Predominantly White, Searchers for a Way to Bring Its Two Divergent Populations Together." *Black Issues in Higher Education,* January 6, p. 30.

Loevy. Robert D., ed. 1998. *The Civil Rights Act of 1964.* Albany: State University of New York Press.

Matthews, F. 1999. "Integration: Speaking the Painful Truth." *Black Issues in Higher Education,* January 7, pp. 24–25.

Mays, Benjamin E. 1960. "Education—To What End?" *Morehouse College Bulletin,* March.

———. 1969. *Disturbed about Man.* Richmond, VA: John Knox.

———. 1971. *Born to Rebel: An Autobiography.* New York: Scribner's; reprint, Athens: University of Georgia Press, 1987.

————. 1978. "The Black College in Higher Education." In *Black Colleges in America: Challenge, Development, Survival,* ed. C. Willie and R. Edmonds, 19–28. New York: Teachers College Press.

————. 2002. "Commencement Address: Twenty-Seven Years of Success and Failure at Morehouse." In *Benjamin E. Mays Speaks,* ed. Freddie C. Colston, 163–174. Lanham, MD: University Press of America.

McBay, S. 1978. "Black Students in the Sciences: A Look at Spelman College." In *Black Colleges in America: Challenge, Development, Survival,* ed. C. Willie and R. Edmonds, 216–228. New York: Teachers College Press.

McCall, N. 1999. *Makes Me Wanna Holler: A Young Black Man in America.* New York: Vintage.

McCall, N., and T. Anderson. 2002. "The Role of Black Colleges in Educating African American Men: An Interview with Nathan McCall." In *Making It on Broken Promises: Leading African American Male Scholars Confront the Culture of Higher Education,* ed. L. Jones and C. West, 113–140. Sterling, VA: Stylus.

Merrill, Charles. 1978. "The Board of Trustees and the Black College." In *Black Colleges in America,* ed. C. Willie and R. Edmonds, 167–174. New York: Teachers College Press.

Merton, Robert K. 1968. *Social Theory and Social Structure.* New York: Free Press; reprint of 1949 edition.

Mitchell, Robert. 1993. *The Multicultural Student's Guide to Colleges.* New York: Noonday Press.

Monro, J. 1978. "Teaching and Learning English." In *Black Colleges in America: Challenge, Development Survival,* ed. C. Willie and R. Edmonds, 235–262. New York: Teachers College Press.

Morehouse College. 1980. *Morehouse College Bulletin* (Winter).

Nabrit, S. M. 1971. "Reflections on the Future of Black Colleges." *Daedalus.*

National Center for Education Statistics. 1996. *Historically Black Colleges and Universities, 1976–1994,* NCES 96902. By Charles Hoffman, Thomas D. Snyder, and Bill Sonnenberg, National Center for Education Statistics, U.S. Department of Education. Washington, DC: U.S. Government Printing Office.

Newby, J. 1982. *Teaching Faculty in Black Colleges and Universities.* Washington, DC: University Press of America.

Nixon, H., and W. Henry. 1992. "White Students at the Black University: Their Experiences Regarding Acts of Racial Intolerance." *Equity and Excellence* 25: 121–123.

Outcalt, C., and T. Skewes-Cox. 2002. "Involvement, Interaction, and Satisfaction: The Human Environment at HBCUs." *Review of Higher Education* 25(3): 331–347.

Pego, D. 1995. "Reaching Out: Hispanic Students Bring Diversity to HBCU." *Black Issues in Higher Education,* December 28, p. 9.

Perez, C. 2002. *The Truth behind the Hype: A Closer Look at the SAT.* Paper presented at the NEACAC Conference, Fairfield University.

Pressley, Samuel W. 1976. "Educator Backs Black Universities." *Evening Bulletin* (Philadelphia), April 26.

Rawls, John. 1971. *A Theory of Justice.* Cambridge: Harvard University Press.

————. 2001. *Justice as Fairness.* Cambridge: Harvard University Press.

Reddick, L. D. 1959. *Crusader Without Violence.* New York: Harper and Brothers.

Riesman, David, and Christopher Jencks. 1968. *The Academic Revolution.* New York: Doubleday.

Rockefeller Foundation. 1968. *President's Five-Year Review and Annual Report.* New York: Rockefeller Foundation.

Roebuck, Julian, and Komanduri S. Murty. 1993. *Historically Black Colleges and Universities.* Westport, CT: Praeger.

Schrader, W. B. 1971. "The Predictive Validity of College Board Admissions Test." In *The College Board Admissions Program,* ed. W. H. Angoff, 195–215. New York: Teachers College Press.

Schumacher, E. F. 1973. *Small Is Beautiful.* New York: Harper and Row.

Shireman, Robert. 2003. "10 Questions College Officials Should Ask about Diversity." *Chronicle of Higher Education,* August 15, pp. B10–B11.

Shores, E. 1979. "The 13th Grade Push." *Change* (October): 31–32.

Sindler, Allan P. 1978. *Bakke, Defunis, and Minority Admissions: The Quest for Equal Opportunity.* New York: Longman.

Smiles, R. 2001. "A World-Class Education: Rewards Abound for Those Who Dare to Teach or Study Abroad." *Black Issues in Higher Education,* August 2, p. 18.

Smith, C. 1978. "Teaching and Learning Social Sciences in Black Universities." In *Black Colleges in America: Challenge, Development, Survival,* ed. C. Willie and R. Edmonds, 195–215. New York: Teachers College Press.

Smith, S. L., and K. W. Borgstedt. 1985. "Factors Influencing Adjustment of White Faculty in Predominantly Black Colleges." *Journal of Negro Education* 54(2): 148–163.

Spelman College. 2003. *Spelman: History in Brief.* Atlanta: Spelman College. http://www.spelman.edu/prospectivestudents/glance/history.html (accessed July 6, 2003).

Standley, Nancy V. 1978. *White Students Enrolled in Black Colleges and Universities.* Atlanta: Southern Regional Board.

Stewart, P. 2001. "Why Xavier Remains No. 1: Louisiana's Xavier University Maintains an Enviable Track Record for Sending More African American Students to Medical School Than Any Other Institution." *Black Issues in Higher Education,* July 19, p. 22.

Tatum, B. D. 1997. *Why Are All the Black Kids Sitting Together in the Cafeteria?* New York: Basic Books.

Thompson, D. 1978. "Black College Faculty and Students: The Nature of Their Interaction." In *Black Colleges in America: Challenge, Development, Survival,* ed. C. Willie and R. Edmonds, 180–194. New York: Teachers College Press.

Tom Joyner Foundation and William J. Clinton Presidential Foundation. 2001. *The Key: An Interactive Guide to Historically Black Colleges and Universities,* Version 1.0 (CD-ROM). New York: Ember Media Corporation.

U.S. Census Bureau. 2002. *Statistical Abstract of the United States.* Washington, DC: U.S. Government Printing Office.

U.S. Department of Education. 2002a. *Digest of Education Statistics, 2002.* Washington, DC: U.S. Government Printing Office.

U.S. Department of Education. 1997. *White House Initiative on Historically Black Colleges and Universities.* Booklet. Washington, DC: U.S. Government Printing Office.

———. 2000. *Digest of Education Statistics, 2000.* Washington, DC: National Center for Education Statistics, U.S. Government Printing Office.

———. 2001. *Digest of Education Statistics, 2001.* Washington, DC: National Center for Education Statistics, U.S. Government Printing Office.

———. 2002a. *Digest of Education Statistics, 2002.* Washington, DC: National Center for Education Statistics, U.S. Government Printing Office.

———. 2002b. *President Bush Signs New Executive Order on HBCUs.* U.S. Department of Education press Release, http://www.ed.gov/PressReleases/022002 /02122002.html (accessed June 26, 2003).

U.S. Department of Labor. 1965. *The Negro Family,* Washington, DC: U.S. Government Printing Office

U.S. Equal Employment Commission. 1975. "Higher Education Staff Information Report (EEO-6)." *National Advisory Committee on Higher Education and Black Colleges and Universities Report,* September 1979, p. 37. Washington, DC: U.S. Government Printing Office.

United Negro College Fund. 1984. *Statistical Report.* New York: United Negro College Fund.

Vars, F., and W. Bowen. 1998. "Scholastic Aptitude Test Scores, Race, and Academic Performance in Selective Colleges and Universities." In *The Black-White Test Score Gap,* ed. C. Jencks and M. Phillips, 457–479. Washington, DC: Brookings.

Verharen, C. 1993. "A Core Curriculum at Historically Black Colleges and Universities: An Immodest Proposal." *Journal of Negro Education* 62(1): 190–203.

Walker, M. 2003. "Jayson Blair Case Prompts New Look at Teaching Ethics." *Black College Wire,* June 4, http://www.blackcollegewire.org/new/030604_ethics/ (accessed September 4, 2003).

Washington, Booker T. 1970. "Industrial Education for the Negro." In *The Black American,* ed. Leslie H. Fishel and Benjamin Quarles, 223–228. Glenview, WI: Scott Foresman.

Wenglinsky H. 1997. *Students at Historically Black Colleges and Universities: Their Aspirations and Accomplishments.* Policy Information Report, ERIC Document Reproduction Service No. ED425239. Princeton, NJ: Educational Testing Service.

Wickham, D. 2003. "Bush Backtracks on Black-College Pledge." *USA Today,* June 2, p. 11A.

Willie, Charles V. 1973. *Race Mixing in the Public Schools.* New York: Praeger.

———. 1978. *The Sociology of Urban Education.* Lexington, MA: Lexington Books of D. C. Heath.

———. 1979. "Black Colleges Redefined." *Change* (October): 46–53.

———. 1981a. *The Ivory and Ebony Towers: Race Relations and Higher Education.* Lexington, MA: Lexington Books.

————. 1981b. "Make It Possible for Whites to Be the Minority: An Educational Goal for the Next Twenty-Five Years." *Negro Educational Review* 32(1) (January): 78–88.

————. 1986. *Five Black Scholars.* Lanham, MD: Abt Books/University Press of America.

————. 1991. "A Social and Historical Context: A Case Study of Philanthropic Assistance." In *The Education of African-Americans,* ed. C. V. Willie, A. M. Garibaldi, and W. L. Reed, 7–24. Westport, CT: Auburn House.

————. 1994a. "Black Colleges Are Not Just For Blacks Anymore." *Journal of Negro Education* 63(2): 153–163.

————. 1994b. *Theories of Human Social Action.* Lanham, MD: Rowman and Littlefield.

Willie, Charles V., and Ronald R. Edmonds, eds. 1978. *Black Colleges in America.* New York: Teachers College Press.

Willie, Charles V., M. Grady, and R. Hope. 1991. *African-Americans and the Doctoral Experience: Implications for Policy.* New York: Teachers College Press.

Willie, Charles V., and C. M. Hedgepeth Jr. 1979. "The Educational Goals of Black Colleges." *Journal of Higher Education* 50(1): 89–96.

Willie, Charles V., and Marlene MacLeish. 1978. "Priorities of Black College Presidents." In *Black Colleges in America,* ed. C. V. Willie and R. Edmonds, 132–148. New York: Teachers College Press.

Willie, Charles V., and Richard J. Reddick. 2003. *A New Look at Black Families,* 5th ed. Walnut Creek, CA: AltaMira Press.

Willie, Sarah Susannah. 2003. *Acting Black.* New York and London: Routledge.

Work, John W. 1940. *American Negro Songs and Spirituals.* New York: Crown, Bonanza.

Wright, Stephen J., B. E. Mays, H. Gloster, and A. W. Dent. 1967. "The American Negro College: Four Responses and a Reply." *Harvard Educational Review* 37(3): 451–467.

Wright, R., and E. Rosskam. 1941. *12 Million Black Voices.* New York: Viking.

Zinn, H. 1970. *The Southern Mystique.* New York: Knopf.